Mama Dip's Family Cookbook

Mama Dip's Family Cookbook

Mildred Council

The University of North Carolina Press

Chapel Hill

Designed by April Leidig-Higgins

Illustrations by Cindy Revell

Set in Monotype Bell by Copperline Book Services

Manufactured in the United States of America

The paper in this book meets the guidelines for permanence and durability of the Committee on Production Guidelines for Book Longevity of the Council on Library Resources.

Library of Congress Cataloging-in-Publication Data

Council, Mildred.

Mama Dip's family cookbook / by Mildred Council.

p. cm.   Includes index.

ISBN 0-8078-2989-7 (cloth: alk. paper)

ISBN 0-8078-5655-x (pbk.: alk. paper)

1. Cookery, American.   2. Mama Dip's Country Kitchen (Restaurant)   I. Title: Family cookbook.

II. Title.

TX15.C8582 2005

641.5973—dc22   2005011751

cloth   09 08 07 06 05   5 4 3 2 1

paper   09 08 07 06 05   5 4 3 2 1

Contents

Acknowledgments

I DEDICATE THIS BOOK to my community. As I look back at the community in Chatham County, North Carolina, where I grew up, I would say it was a community of farmers, including my Papa, who was a single parent rearing seven children in the time of the Great Depression. During this time, the cutworms and boll weevils ate the cotton, the fox ate the chickens, and the snakes ate the hen's eggs, but everybody worked, laughed, and played. We never heard the word "poverty" or "poor" unless we were skinny. The women in the community at church made quilts, sheets, and clothes to share with Papa. We all felt cared for. What this community gave us didn't come in a box wrapped with ribbon. It came in words and deeds.

Papa was soft-spoken, and every word had its meaning. He dedicated his life to his promise to my Mama, who died when I was a baby, to raise the children. Many times after supper he would tell us about how things had always gotten better for him and Mama and that things would be good for us too. He often sang the spiritual "God's Gonna Trouble the Water So Look Away to the Kingdom." I believe the "kingdom" was the community where people shared their time and talents with us.

This book is also dedicated to my children, grandchildren, and great-grandchildren. To my children: thank you for knowing that work is part of life's struggles. Thank you for teaching your children important life skills. To my grandchildren: remember all of the life and cooking skills that you learned and pass them on to my great-grandchildren. Always remember the holidays when we came together as a family and talked about growing up, along with all the lessons you learned from your Sunday school teachers, schoolteachers, football coaches, and many others.

I have found that my writing group has come together again to work on this cookbook, and I want to thank so many people for helping me to write a second book—Judie Birchfield for editing and assisting me, turning so many pages over and over again; Joe Nathan Council for baking the desserts and making sure that the recipes are accurate; Annette Council for typing up all the recipes; Spring Council for assisting with all the recipes; Tom Finn and Chelsea Birchfield-Finn for taking pictures of me and my restaurant for the book. I want to thank all of them for their patience and for helping me when I struggled to remember many of the recipes that I have cooked over the years in different places and different jobs. I want to thank the employees at Mama Dip's for making sure that the restaurant continued to be "me" while I was away traveling with the first cookbook and for keeping the food going out with the same level of quality as if I had never set foot out of the kitchen. I also want to thank the UNC Press for suggesting that I put together this second cookbook.

I would also like to say thanks to Sandra, Geary, Annette, Joe, Tonya, Stephanie, Spring, and Evan for choosing to make Mama Dip's a family business. I'd like to thank the children for all of their specific contributions to the business. Food has always been at the heart of our family. My daughter Elaine is the general manager of the restaurant. Annette worked for the town of Carrboro for years but never really left Mama Dip's and now is the full-time company accountant and business manager. Geary sold furniture in Charlotte for eight years but also worked in food, and then he came back to cook in Mama Dip's kitchen. Joe Nathan is the baker in the business. Tonya is a waitress and dining room supervisor. Evan has been working in the kitchen since he was 11 years old. He assists the waitstaff in cutting and putting up the desserts. Stephanie is the cashier, and she takes all the party orders and take-out orders. Spring has been a cashier and assistant to Elaine and Annette.

William has his own business in Charlotte, North Carolina, but also cooks for the community. My oldest daughter, Norma, started Little Teddies Daycare, and my daughter Julia owns Bon's BBQ restaurant in Carrboro.

I also want to thank Eugene, Kenny, Emanuel, Robert, Della, and Andrea for choosing Mama Dip's restaurant for your career for the past 18 years. We are all in the family. May God forever bless you. Thank you to Della for being one of the best cooks in the kitchen next to me. To all the students who have worked at the restaurant: I hope Mama Dip's has helped to meet your needs, even if it was just with mashed potatoes and two pieces of white meat chicken, while you were at the University of North Carolina. I enjoyed all of your willingness to work without worrying about the issue of race. One of the things the students first learned was to follow the rules. It is an educational process for them to work some while they're still young, and they meet people and learn how to deal with them. A restaurant is good for that.

I want to thank people who wrote after reading the first cookbook to share their stories of country life and laugh about things that we all did on the farm. Now that we are older we see the deer coming into our backyards in town, where we used to see them in the cornfields in the country. Good luck to all of you in your cooking.

I am a known "dump cook," having come up in the late 1930s and 1940s —measuring cups and spoons were not available at my house. I have found from getting calls and letters from people all over the United States that some recipes work well in some areas and don't work so well in other areas. So I suggest to you to make the recipe as you would a skirt—make it to your size and taste and never throw it out. If it's meat, add gravy. If it's a dessert, add sauce and ice cream and serve it. Just make it pretty, and thank you for your suggestions.

Finally, I am grateful to my team of workers. Thanks to you all— wherever you may be. I hope life is serving you well.

Mama Dip's Family Cookbook

Introduction

We All Felt Cared For

IN MY FIRST BOOK, *Mama Dip's Kitchen*, I talked about growing up on a farm in Chatham County, North Carolina, with my brothers and sisters. Farming wasn't called a career then, but we learned how to prepare the fields, plant, chop, pick, harvest, and cook the food that we grew. We milked the cows, fed the pigs and the chickens, and churned our own butter. We used a mule for help on the farm. Papa wouldn't let us have a horse because he said horses were too frisky for us.

After moving to Chapel Hill, I went to a beauty school in Durham. I never wanted to go to beauty school, but after my Papa begged me to go, I went. I lived with my grandmother while I was in school. What I really wanted to do was to cook because I loved to cook. My brother and sister were both cooking at the time, and I wanted to, also. So, my first job after I got out of beauty school was cooking for the Patterson family over on Wilson Court in Chapel Hill. Later, I cooked at the Carolina Coffee Shop and at various places around the University of North Carolina, including fraternity houses, and then I worked at Bill's Barbeque for 18 years.

I gave birth to my first child in 1949 and my last in 1957. I had become the mother of eight—five girls and three boys. (In the fifties, it wasn't unusual for people to have big families.) We had a hard time finding a house with three bedrooms. We finally moved into a house in the Northside community of Chapel Hill and lived there for nine years. We had a wood cookstove and wood heater. My house was no different from those of most of the other families we knew. The children took turns sleeping on the couch and floor. In the winter months, it was a struggle to put food on the table and buy wood and coal for the stove to keep warm.

I was always the main breadwinner. When my husband got out of the army after World War II, the only job he could find was in the sawmill. When it rained or snowed, he couldn't work. So I worked two jobs and ironed clothes for students on campus. I also washed and curled hair for neighbors and friends (using what I learned at the beauty school).

Despite our struggles, there have been so many things to laugh about —like when a card table suddenly collapsed and spilled all of the food on the floor. One year my oldest daughter, Norma, collected money from everyone and bought my first watch from the pawnshop at Five Points in Durham. Later, the children began giving me different kinds of salt and pepper shakers. Another year I said I knew what gifts would be good for my birthday and Christmas gifts, and I picked a china pattern at the Belks department store and asked for pieces. After I got so many nice pieces, my granddaughter Stephanie and I decided to start a china club for those in the family with homes of their own. After Norma got her china I don't know what happened, but our china club was sort of forgotten. Maybe it was Mama Dip's that we all got wrapped up in.

In 1976 I was walking down the street when George Tate, who was the first black realtor in town, stopped me and asked me to take over a failing restaurant that was leasing some space in one of his buildings. My first re-action was "What? I have no money!" Well, I did have $64, so I thought it over and then used that money to buy the food for the first meal. I bought Pine Sol and wax to clean the old restaurant; bacon, eggs, grits, flour, bread, instant coffee, and Pet milk to cook breakfast; and Joy detergent to wash the dishes. After I made money from that first meal, I went right out and bought the ingredients for the second one, and we served dinner that evening. We've been open ever since.

In the beginning we had 18 seats, and then after nine months we moved things around to make room for 22 seats. After taking down a wall, we grew to 38 seats. Later we were able to rent the other side of the building, and we grew to 94 seats. The seating grew but the kitchen did not, which caused us to have a slowdown in service. We wrote out a different, new menu every day, and I realized that it was difficult to keep that up. I began to wonder about myself. The hours at the beginning were from seven A.M. to one A.M. At first, I did not realize how many hours I was working, but then I had never worked only one job at a time. Later, we changed the hours to eight A.M. to ten P.M. and also fixed a standard menu. Life settled down, and in 1997, I began to think about building a new, bigger build-

The sign that hangs outside of Mama Dip's Kitchen at 408 West Rosemary Street in Chapel Hill, North Carolina. This sign hung outside the old restaurant, located across the street, as well. Photograph by Chelsea Birchfield-Finn.

ing across the way at 408 West Rosemary Street. I started the process of buying the land and building a new restaurant with a parking lot. Around the same time, many of my customers and my friends, including Alice Welch and Bill Neal, were encouraging me to publish my recipes. So I began to write a cookbook.

In the early part of 1998, the magazine *Southern Living* wrote an article about my restaurant and me. It was published on Memorial Day weekend, May 31, 1998, and it drew a huge crowd to the restaurant. We could barely feed all the people who came to Mama Dip's Kitchen that weekend. We closed at 11 P.M. and got most people served by 1 A.M. People also tasted the Mama Dip's prepared food we had for sale, and they wanted to know all about my jellies and about my garden too, which was mentioned in *Southern Living*.

Around Thanksgiving time of that same year, ABC's *Good Morning America* called and talked to my daughter Elaine about my appearing on their

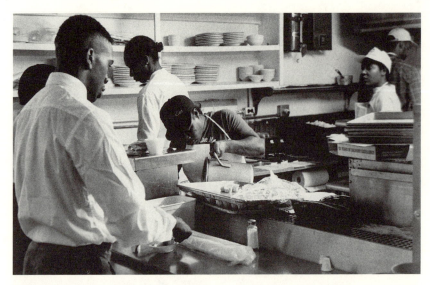
Members of the Council family working in the kitchen of the old restaurant on a busy Sunday morning, 1980. Photograph by Tiffany Prather.

show. She was so excited that she told one of my other daughters, Annette, who suggested that she tell them yes for me. However, when I heard about all this, I said I didn't really want to go to New York for Thanksgiving. My kids said, "Mama, you have to do it!" but I told ABC I didn't want to come. So ABC said they would come to Chapel Hill instead and set up a feature on my cooking right on the UNC campus.

When word got out about this, a chef at a local Chapel Hill restaurant called to ask me if I was looking for a food stylist. I answered, "No, I have never heard of a 'food stylist.'" He was pleased to let me know that he was one. I really didn't know what to say but told him, "Maybe *Good Morning America* is looking for someone, but not me, sir." After I hung up the phone, I was so puzzled. I began to think, "What would they do to style collards, potatoes, cornbread, and other country food?" Maybe he was kidding me. I thought that hair and clothes probably needed a stylist, but not food. I later learned that there really is such a person as a food stylist.

The news got around somehow that I needed a food stylist. A woman

Joe Nathan Council cleaning up the old restaurant at the end of the day, 1979. Photograph by Tiffany Prather.

called from Raleigh, introduced herself as a food stylist, and said she would like to come to Chapel Hill to meet me. I said OK and waited to see what she wanted from me.

When the food stylist arrived at Mama Dip's, she said she would be happy to work with me and with the food for ABC's show. We talked about the food that I would prepare and about exactly where and when the taping would take place on the UNC campus. She had some pretty bowls and baking dishes for us to use. Along with the pecan pie, I was to have some fried chicken, ham, collards, yams, cornbread, and coconut cake already made. ABC asked me to make a pecan pie during the taping of the show with Spencer Christian. It was truly an experience having Mr. Christian help me stir! It was also great fun to be on TV so early in the morning.

We all had a good time on UNC's campus with Spencer Christian and the ABC *Good Morning America* staff, as well as the students on campus who got up early in the morning to be part of the show. We could feel the dew on our feet as we walked on the grass, and my whole body got chilled, but the thrill of being there with Spencer Christian and ABC kept me warm. The food stylist made the food look like a picture in a book. I loved it. I was really worried about how my pecan pie would come out. It turned out to be really great.

On February 1, 1999, we moved into our new location across West Rosemary Street from the old restaurant, where we had been for 23 years, and then in the fall of that year *Mama Dip's Kitchen* was published. The past five years since then have been more than I could ever have imagined. Now, looking back, I wonder how I made it through the first years, and I realize that Mama Dip's Kitchen and Mildred "Mama Dip" Council grew up together. Now I am in my seventies, have my restaurant in a new building, am still making jellies, pickles, and chow-chow, and have written a second cookbook. I have never looked back until now.

I HAD NEVER imagined that I would publish a book or that a national TV network would call and invite me on their show. I had always thought of myself as a simple country girl. What did I have? I was born on a farm in Chatham County and raised there by my Papa with my four sisters and two brothers. My Mama had passed on in 1931. She wanted her children to grow up together. So, with the oldest child about 12 and me about 2, Papa took on the challenge of raising us all together when the economy was at its lowest point—the Great Depression. He was a great Papa—a steward, cook, teacher, farmer, and motivator for all of us! He taught us life skills.

Growing up on the farm, we learned to plant, chop, pick, shell, can, fish, and hunt—and to cook all of the things we grew and caught. My sisters and brothers and I found joy in so many things. For fun we jumped rope and played jack rocks, baseball, and learning games. We also always challenged each other—who could jump rope the longest or hit the ball the farthest or pick more cotton. We always wanted to talk about what we accomplished at the supper table.

Farm life was all about community. Farming friends and relatives shared the same concerns and values—working hard together, going to

Mama Dip's Kitchen. Photograph by Chelsea Birchfield-Finn.

school and to church, and helping each other when needed. We shared each other's struggles and were told stories about challenges and how to overcome them. We went to school, but college was never mentioned as an option for us at that time. However, people would tell me how my mother had gone away to college to learn to be a teacher and that when she came back she wore these pretty blouses and skirts. That was quite unusual in those days!

Every year for many years, Papa planted nine acres of cotton in long rows up and down hills on a tenant farm. When I was young I was given a short-handled hoe and shorter rows to work on at chopping time in the late spring. Late August, September, and October were cotton-picking time. The younger children would get a feed sack to fill with the cotton. Once we were eight years old, our sacks got bigger. At the beginning of picking season it was a lot of fun, but as the season wore on our backs became so tired. Papa kept our spirits up by bringing special goodies from town. When he sold some cotton, he would bring back cocoa for hot chocolate, peppermint and horehound sticks, and Coca-Cola for us to share.

I loved to plow the fields with our mule, Joe, who was very gentle. All we had to say was "giddiup Joe" and he would go. We would say "har" and Joe would go right and then "gee" to have him go left, and we said "woo" to make him stop. At the end of the day after plowing, I would look back at the field and think it really looked pretty. Plowing was much easier than chopping.

I plowed until the warplanes started zooming overhead during World War II. Strange trucks started passing by, too. Some people said that soldiers dressed in funny-looking uniforms were camping down on the nearby Haw River. One Sunday, Papa stood up in church and told the ladies of the congregation that they should be like "mother birds" and get up early to help boys who were going off to war. We knew little about the war—only that the authorities drafted men from ages 18 to 45. When our family's turn came, my brothers left home for the army and the navy, and they didn't come back home to the farm before Papa and I moved to Chapel Hill.

When the war was going on Uncle Sam took all our men. It seemed that no men were left, just boys with raggedy britches who wore "turn-over" shoes (shoes that were worn down on one side) and faded overalls that were patched on the butt and knees. Papa would go to other farms to get boys to help us on our farm. When they would come to our farm, they would just stare at me as if they were saying, "What are you doing out here?" I challenged all of them. "Are you going to work or just stand there and look at me, you lazy things?" I said.

I always had to stop playing and tie the mule to a tree or bush at the spring to get fresh water for the lazy boys. We didn't have a well and used a spring to get our water. I wanted to take the boys with me so I could push them onto the snake that always hung around the spring. When I saw the snake, I would chunk rocks and sticks until it slid away. The spring was down a little hill, and I would kneel on a piece of plank placed next to it to dip the water out into a bucket. Most of the time the bucket would be a gallon Jewell lard bucket. The dipper was a big gourd that Papa cut the top out of and then cleaned out the seeds. Later, Papa could afford a galvanized dipper.

Sometimes when we were in the fields, the galvanized dipper would spring a leak, and it would be a long time before Papa could get another one. We would just drink from the broken one, with water coming out of the hole. When aluminum dippers came into the store, Papa bought one, but the handle didn't stay on it long, and then we just started using a blue and white pot. I liked to drink the water and let it run down from my mouth onto my dress or onto the ground when it was hot in the field.

We planted cotton, corn, wheat, oats, rye, and sugarcane. We also had a garden in a special place near the house. We planted our early vegetables there—onions, cabbage, and English peas in January and February, Irish potatoes in late March, and string beans and field peas around Good Friday, the week before Easter. Sweet potatoes were the last thing that we planted in the spring. Papa and most all the farmers had a cedar post hanging high with gourds to scare the crows away from the gardens. Sometimes smaller birds would lay their eggs in the gourds in the springtime.

At the house, our inside broom was made of wild straw that grew three feet tall in the fields. We had to wring off the roots. This means we would twist the straw from the roots, turning it until the roots broke off and we were left with a handful of straw. In the fall, after the frost, we would clean off the leaves left on the straw and wrap a twine string around the top of the broom to make a handle. It would be bushy, and we would cut off the tip to even it across. The brooms always stood beside the wood box or the fireplace. The yard broom was made of dogwood limbs or branches. The limbs would have to be cut off the tree and pulled straight. Four to five limbs would be tied together. One person would hold them together while the other would tie them. Sometimes we used corn shucks stuck in a piece of oak wood for our outside broom. Using a bracing bit, we made holes in the wood and pushed in the corn shucks. Our mop was made of burlap sacks tied around a hoe.

We had lye soap for washing, and we had something called "bluing" for rinsing our clothes. It made the water a pretty blue color. The biggest washtub was used for bathing on Saturday nights. We used sweet or Octagon soap for bathing, and we took turns in the washtub. After we were age ten or so we had to put the middle part of our body into the washtub first when getting in, then the rest would follow. For some reason the tub seemed smaller!

Papa built what was called a hothouse for raising chickens. Back then, many farmers talked about how much money they made raising and selling fryers. Our hothouse could hold 500 chicks. Papa would go somewhere in nearby Pittsboro and order baby chicks that were all the same color and size. When they came in, they were so pretty, chirping and eating. A lantern had to be put in the hothouse so that the chicks could eat any time during the day or night. We had to keep food and water in their trays all the time. The chickens grew fast. In three or four months they would weigh up to three pounds. Someone would come in a big truck with coops to take them away. We had to catch them by their legs and count them while we put them in the coop. Then the hothouse was cleaned out, new sawdust was added, and then here came more baby chicks. I liked it when we got food in exchange for the chickens. Other times we would exchange them for pretty socks printed with checks or flowers.

Most of the women in the community earned money by taking in washing. That's what they called it. They were washing and ironing for white people. The men's collars and cuffs were supposed to be stiff. The starch was made from flour and water boiled until almost clear. The sheets would be slick as glass, folded evenly and put in a basket to be delivered or picked up by the man of the house.

When corn-shucking time came in late summer, the black women had to go help the white women cook, and the white men would come help to shuck Papa's corn. When the women had dinner ready, the white men would eat first. Then the black men ate. The children ate last. That was the way it was on every farm. The word segregation never came up. The white people called Papa "Uncle Ed." This exchange of labor was part of the people in the community sharing their skills with each other. No one paid anyone else for it.

About every three months, two men came around selling special goods. The Watkins flavoring man had a creamy vanilla flavoring and whole nutmeg that we had to scrape with a knife for our egg custard. The lemon flavoring that he sold was good in apple pie or cobbler. The vanilla was put on dried apples for fried pies—though they weren't actually fried.

They were grilled in an oblong cast-iron pan shaped like a platter. It had two big holes at each end that we used as a handle. When we weren't using it, we hung it on the wall behind the stove over the wood box.

The kids really didn't like anything the Watkins man sold but his flavoring. He also sold black draught, Epsom salt, barcum worm killer (my, oh my, it was bad stuff), and cod-liver oil that seemed to have come straight from the fish—not even diluted. He sold clover leaf ointment that we put on our legs after we sat too close to the fire. All the girls got polka-dotted legs in the winter from sitting too close to the fireplace in the cold early mornings. Sparks would fly out of the fireplace and burn our skin. We would all stand around the fireplace and could warm only our fronts until the fire really got started. When breakfast was ready, we had to warm our plates over the kitchen fire or stove before putting the food on them in winter. If we didn't do this, the molasses and butter and gravy would sit like pancakes on the cold plate.

The other salesman was the hair-dressing man. We called him the Sweetheart Man. He sold "Sweetheart and Dolly Dimple" hair grease, coconut shampoo, and tar shampoo. Tar shampoo was supposed to help cure the ringworm that some children had. Ringworm looked like a little white-gray spot where mounds of hair would fall out. It was really hard to cure. Papa said that those children who had it weren't getting enough to eat. Our family never had ringworms.

The Sweetheart Man also sold us big hair-straightening combs that we warmed on the corner of the cookstove. Then we would take the mirror from the wall, prop it on the flour can, and made ourselves pretty. We would part our hair in the style we liked and twist and roll locks of our hair with strips of brown paper bags. We would sleep with the rolls in our hair overnight and take them out in the morning for school or church. Sometimes our hair would be twisted with thread or plaited in cornrows or braided.

I was real tender-headed. Jeanette Burnette, our neighbor across the creek, was the only one who ever combed my hair after Mama died. She would twist my hair in threads, and, my family said, I just didn't want anyone else bothering my head.

When I was five, my father cut off all my hair. It was long past my shoulder, and I wouldn't let it be washed in the first May water. (In the spring, the first May water was caught in a can, and it was like gold in every household. Everybody washed their hair in it.) So Papa asked me whether I wanted any hair. I shook my head and told him, "No, sir." He said, "Just sit there until I come back."

I will never forget the slender, silver scissors and the shiny clippers with two handles that he carried back. He began to put the hair that he cut in my lap. The clippers skinning my head hurt. Soon I had no hair. My hair actually grew back fast, but Papa said he would not cut it any more. He said I would have to let Jeanette Burnette cut my hair after that. Jeanette remained my good friend, and we continued to see each other for many, many years until she died.

No one could believe how fast I was growing. I always had big feet. Papa would put half-soles and heels on our shoes when we wore a hole in them or nail the toes back down if the leather came loose. He had two shoe horses—one that had two sizes and one tall one—that were kept in a back room. He would buy sheets of leather, mark out the piece needed, lick the nails, and knock them in. Then he would trim the leather, file the edges smooth, and put taps on the heel and toe. He would take a pair of my brother Jim's shoes and put taps all around the shoe sole, and then we would clap for one another and buck dance or tap dance on Sunday afternoons like Papa had taught us.

We used to place a piece of paper over a comb to make a harp and dance. We all could dance. Susie Q and Truckin' were dances we all learned. Now kids do a dance called the Chicken that is similar to Truckin.' We learned dancing from our older sisters. One year someone brought a Victrola home. We would wind it up, put the needle on, and play those blues, sad songs, and gospel quartets.

Country life for Papa in Chatham County was a lot of work and very little play. Still, I sometimes look back and think that those were the better days, because we didn't work on Sunday and Saturday evening was time to prepare for Sunday and to play.

The neighbors' children were always at our house on Saturday to play. Late in the day I would hear our neighbors calling to their children from across the meadow branch, "You had better come on home!" (The meadow branch was the creek that ran between the Burnette and Cotton family farms.) We made many things to play with. The bean shooters we used were usually made from dogwood limbs, but sometimes we used oak limbs. If we wanted a pretty one, we would cut it to look like a "Y" with two prongs and a handle. Then we cut the tongues out of old shoes and cut strips out of old inner tubes. We would make a hole in each end of the leather shoe tongues and tie the rubber strips to the leather. Then, using strong thread, we would tie the leather and rubber to the prongs. We called them slingshots, and they were dangerous. My brothers could knock out a chicken or a bird with one.

Another thing that we made for playing was a wagon. I learned how strong oak was and the difference between red oak and white oak trees for making parts for the wagon. Our neighbor, Boy Baldwin, would saw two wheels from the big end of the tree and two wheels from the smaller end. We made a shallow hole in the backyard and let it fill with rainwater in which we soaked and seasoned the wood. We let it soak in the hole for days with a rock on top so it would not warp.

Using the bracing bit like a chisel, we bored a hole in the center of all four wheels. Then we took off the bark and shaved both sets of wheels into the same size. We made the axle out of wood from a white oak tree, shaving it with old, broken glass until it was slick as glass. In the evening, while we were sitting by the fire or doing nothing we would put the wagon together, make a bed for it, and tie rope that was too worn to use on the mules around the axle to get it ready to roll down Buckner's Hill in the springtime. We used to guide it with our feet. Through the winter the old wagon would be worn out from hauling wood from the woodpile to put on the porch, but we would fix it up again the next spring.

We all caught spring lizards and tadpoles and often made what we called a Ginny hole to put them in. We played with them in the hole. We also made a bigger Ginny hole for swimming. To make this, we would move the rocks and dirt near the creek by hand until we had a hole. The hole would fill up when it rained, and sometimes the creek would fill it in also. Then we would go swimming. I never could swim well. We had to close our eyes while the others got in and out of the hole because we didn't have swimming suits.

The creek and Ginny hole got us all in trouble one time or another because we would get playing with each other and forget the time. I would listen for some parent to holler, "Y'all better come on home and get in some wood" (or "milk" or "feed"). If we were called too often and didn't come back in time, our parents would meet us with a switch. At every lick we would be asked if we were going to do it again. Sometimes we would go home with our friends while they got their switching, and sometimes they would come home with us while we got ours.

Papa could never really whip us. My brother Jim wanted to get his licks first so he would lie on his back and slide around and holler. Papa would look at us and say, "If Effie were here, she would tear y'all to pieces" (Effie was my mother's name). But Papa just didn't have the nerve to whip us. So often, he would instead remember and chuckle about the silly things he did growing up and then let us go.

We entertained ourselves at home together as a family. We had a battery-run radio that Papa would turn on when it was time for *Fibber McGee and Molly, Amos and Andy, Lum and Abner,* and the boxing matches. We would all sit around the kitchen table and make sounds — patting our hips and chests to sound like a horse trotting, for example.

My Aunt Laura and Uncle Jim lived about six miles from us. Uncle Jim was my Papa's brother, and he and Laura didn't have any children. We went to their home often after church. Since my Mama had died, Papa asked Aunt Laura to tell us about where babies came from. Aunt Laura talked to me about womanhood. All the older people were telling their children the same thing — that babies came from a stump in the woods. When one of the women had a baby, they would send their other children to play with us until the baby was born. Back then, new mothers didn't get out of bed for nine days after birth. The room would remain dark, and other women from the community would come to care for the new mother, the baby, and the house and to do the cooking, too. After nine days, the children would finally see the baby. And then we would go looking for that stump. We never found one.

When I had my first child I felt that Papa had let me down by letting

Aunt Laura tell me this. She had never birthed a child. Unlike today, back then we weren't taught the truth about womanhood and birthing.

Growing up in the country certainly taught me how to handle many of life's struggles, but I'm not sure I was quite prepared to be on national TV when I was close to 70 years old. As it turned out, *Good Morning America* was just the beginning.

AFTER THE University of North Carolina Press published my first cookbook, *Mama Dip's Kitchen*, in 1999, I was asked to appear on the Food Network show *Cooking Live with Sara Moulton*. I couldn't believe it! The UNC Press staff told me that I had to go to New York on an airplane to appear on the show. I thought, "To New York — you have got to be kidding me! Flying is not my kind of ride, you know, and all that walking, too!" I needed to think about it. I didn't know what exactly I needed to think about, just that I had to think. In just a few days they wanted me to go to New York and stay in the Paramount Hotel. I had read about this hotel and the movie stars that stayed there. I couldn't believe I would be going to stay in that hotel.

They said that someone would come pick me up at the hotel and take me to the place where Sara filmed her TV show. They wanted me to cook live on TV. I was excited and happy about the possibility of being in New York City, but the airplane ride was still weighing on my mind. I felt shaky. My daughter Elaine told me that I should just get on the plane, get an aisle seat, and shut my eyes. That's it. Well, I won't say any more, but I decided to go.

We arrived in New York, and I was taken to the studio, where I was supposed to get ready for the show. I met the makeup stylist, a young lady. She asked me to sit on a little stool and then she began applying makeup. After she finished, I said to myself, "Maybe I should ask for samples of that makeup!" I was so surprised that she had covered all the moles on my face. All I could think to say was, "Look at me, no moles. Where did they go?"

A representative from UNC Press went with me to tape the TV show, and afterward we went out to dinner. I am sure that everyone at the restaurant

Mama Dip autographing her first book, *Mama Dip's Kitchen*. Photograph by Tom Finn.

thought that my face was natural. When I got back to the hotel, I began to prepare for bed and took a shower. The water began to turn brown. I washed and rinsed several times. All the towels and wash clothes were brown, and I was sure that I had finally gotten all the make up off. The next morning I noticed that the pillowcases were brown. And still all my moles weren't there. When I get back home, for days people would ask, "Who did your face?" I couldn't see one mole. I got many compliments about my makeup. People said that it looked great! I did feel good about myself.

My first trip to *Cooking Live with Sara Moulton* was quite an experience for me, since it was my first time cooking in a TV studio kitchen with a gourmet chef. First, I had to feel good about myself. I was worried because I am 6'2" and Sara is only 5'. I had to figure out how to talk, hear her, and look at the camera all at the same time. For a 70-year-old, it was something really, really new. It was like something coming out of the sky— you weren't expecting it. Sara and I cooked a good meal, and I enjoyed it.

The main dining room of Mama Dip's Kitchen. Photograph by Chelsea Birchfield-Finn.

We made chicken, fried green tomatoes, and sweet potato biscuits. The UNC Press made a tape of it, but to date I haven't looked at it.

A year later, Sara Moulton called and said that she wanted to cook with me again. When she called, I wasn't home, so she left a message that she wanted to come to my *house* to cook in my kitchen. When I got this news, the first thing that popped into my mind was a list of what I would need to do to get ready for her to come here. Suddenly I realized that I had just two days until she arrived, so I stopped running in circles and thought, just let her come and we'll work it out when she gets here.

Sara arrived in Chapel Hill, bringing her camera and staff with her. At 8:30 in the morning, the makeup lady knocked at the door. Nobody had told me that a makeup lady was coming. She needed a place to make us up, so I fixed up my bathroom, put a pillow on the commode, and that's where I sat for my makeup. About 8:45 A.M., the food stylist arrived. She had her dishes and things that she wanted to cook, so we found space in our little kitchen.

Joe Nathan Council baking pecan pies. Photograph by Tom Finn.

Suddenly the doorbell rang, and it was Sara Moulton. She acted as if we had worked together everyday, although it had been a year since we had cooked together on her show. The taping was an all-day thing. We cooked pie and made piecrusts for Sara's new show, *Sara's Secrets.*

Later, we walked around my neighborhood on Martha's Lane and talked about different things—everyday conversation about food and such. Then we ate at Mama Dip's Kitchen. We had a good day that lasted from 9 A.M. to 7 P.M.

After Sara Moulton came to my home, the *700 Club* called and said they wanted to do a documentary on me. I agreed, and the producer came to the restaurant and spent the day with us. He interviewed me about my life and got many of the details of my childhood. Then they made a film of my life. The interviewer played my Papa, and his daughter played me in the film. When I saw this tape, it brought tears to my eyes.

After *Good Morning America* and *Cooking Live with Sara Moulton*, people began calling from local TV stations. I could not imagine what was happening. What had I done to get all this attention? I had been cooking this same country food for many years. What was going on here? It was one call after another. I was so surprised.

Then the QVC home shopping network asked me to come on their channel to sell books, and so I flew to Philadelphia with a UNC Press representative. I was shaking because flying was still not my favorite ride. The pilot handled the flight well, and it went okay.

After the long ride in a big, celebrity-style limo, we got to the QVC headquarters, and the staff there geared me up and escorted me to the TV area. The host for my segment, David Venable, introduced me to the TV viewing public, displayed some of my food, which had been prepared for the show by a food stylist, and talked about my cookbook. After a few minutes the bold electronic sign read, "Sold Out," and the staff escorted me back to the studio guest room. All the books were gone.

In the guest room, there were TVs and counting machines that showed us how many books had been sold on QVC that day. I sat down—everyone was clapping and celebrating. I really didn't feel that there was anything to be happy about. I felt alone. That's when I asked for a drink. I felt that I needed something stronger than a Coke. Well, they served only sodas. But after a few minutes I was ok. I guess I had been a bit nervous.

I appeared on QVC 19 more times to sell my *Mama Dip's Kitchen* cookbook. A representative from my publisher was always able to go with me to these shows. I was beginning to be OK on a plane—but then came September 11, 2001, and flying became a lot harder. The two-hour wait in each airport was not so bad, but the planes seemed to get smaller. I would think to myself, "Oh, my goodness—for goodness sake. I can hardly buckle my seat belt, but I will be ok."

My first time on a UNC public television fund-raiser was interesting. I asked my daughter Spring to drive me to the station and assist me. I cooked fried chicken prior to leaving and put it in a new Pyrex casserole dish. At the studio, I set my dish on a burner in an area behind the stage. Somebody at the fund-raiser forgot to turn the burner off. I was about to be introduced with Bob Garner, the North Carolina barbecue and country cooking author, and then Spring was supposed to bring the chicken in from the back. But about four to five minutes into the show, we heard

Mama Dip at the QVC network studio in Pennsylvania, discussing her pecan pies with food stylist Anthony Corrado in 2001. Photograph by Gina Mahalek.

a big bang—the sound of an explosion. It was my chicken going every-where. The Pyrex casserole dish had overheated and blown up. Thank-fully, we weren't on live TV yet. It ended up working out fine because I had brought another chicken with me. Later that evening the situation seemed funnier that it had when we were on the show.

After *Good Morning America* had put me on the map, I was asked to visit 56 places in 2001, including schools, libraries, community groups, and so on. I am often asked to give food donations for community proj-ects and children's groups. Most of my donations are chicken drumettes or chicken wings. When someone calls and says that they are having a meeting and would like a donation, chicken wings come to mind. I have cooked many chicken wings for so many people. I enjoy doing it because I believe in people helping people, and it is one way for me to give joy back to the community.

When bookstore owners ask me to come speak at book signings, I always write a speech. Then I forget to look at it or leave it at home, so I

Geary Wayne Council slicing apples for pie. Photograph by Tom Finn.

end up just telling stories about myself, Mama Dip's, and the community where I grew up. Everyone tells me that they like to hear my stories because they can imagine the scene so clearly or, sometimes, even remember what I'm describing, whether it is picking cotton or milking the cow, the aprons people wore in the kitchen or the spread on the tables at community dinners. These are country things that people love to hear about. We walk around everyday not realizing that what we did with our time back in 1930s and 1940s was so different than it is today with all the technology and things that people have.

When I go to the schools to talk about my business, the kids ask me about the money part. They always want to know how much money people can make in a restaurant before they ask me about the work part. We have a lot of fun figuring out how much money I might make. For example, if I bought a chicken for this price and sold it for that price, how much money would I make? It is sort of like a word problem for the class to work out.

SCHOOLS WERE VERY different when I was growing up. We had one teacher for grades one through eight, and we were all in the same room together. I would end up learning to spell all the words that the eighth graders knew well before I was in the eighth grade. At school every morning we had to say the Lord's Prayer and sing a certain song:

Good morning to you.
Good morning to you.
We are all in our places with sunshiny faces,
And this is the way to start a new day.

Then we recited the Pledge of Allegiance and sang "God Bless America." I remember the words:

God bless America,
Land that I love.
Stand beside her, and guide her
Through the night with a light from above.
From the mountains, to the prairies,
To the oceans, white with foam.
God bless America, my home sweet home.

In December, school would get out for Christmas. Our teachers, Miss Smith and Miss Maggie Atkins, would make hot chocolate on the stove at the school, and my sister Bernice would make big molasses cookies that were cut out with empty Luzianne coffee tins or a bowl. Each student would have to bring some milk or sugar for the hot cocoa. Miss Atkins would push the desks back, and we would all sit on the floor in a circle. She would tell us about when she was a little girl in school and what she got for Christmas when she was young. She would ask us what we wanted Santa to bring us, and she would write to Santa for the good students and write to the parents of the ones that could do better for Santa next year.

The teachers checked the "roll" to see how many days one had been absent from school before Christmas. Fall was harvest time in the country for the cotton and corn, and harvesting just had to be done by family members. If a neighborhood family's children had to stay out of school for the harvest, we would always tell them what we had learned in school, and we would get together and play teacher. We played learning games like spelling bees, with different people taking turns calling out the words. While keeping the yard clean, we worked out arithmetic problems with a dried dogwood or pine limb. Sometimes we missed days of school, but we made sure not to miss learning. We were friends and neighbors helping each other. Papa would bring us candy sticks and cheese and crackers as prizes for helping each other. We would also make molasses candy and roast peanuts in the oven, and we would pop and roast corn for prizes.

If a teacher told a child's parents that their child was behind, we would help that child with chores so that he or she could catch up on studying. We would put the name of the chore in someone's cap and shake it up. One person would sit in a chair with a blindfold on. Someone else would stand in front of them holding the cap. Then the person standing would say, "Heavy, heavy is hanging over your head, is it a lady or gent? What must I do to win this prize?" The seated person would pull out a chore from the cap and read what it said. Along with the chores, there would also be things such as "Say moo like a cow," "Call out spelling words," "Help read," or "Help with arithmetic" or other subjects. We got a prize for helping, and we helped a child who needed it every chance we got.

We also had Easter and Children's Day poems to learn for church, plus school poems. No one wanted anyone to be punished with the switch, so we had fun wishing, hoping, thinking, and helping one another.

By the time I was old enough for high school, the school bus had begun picking up the children in our community to go to Horton High School in Pittsboro. All the girls learned how to make broomstick skirts, sewing them by hand. (Broomstick skirts were made out of chicken feed sacks and gathered snug around the waistband so that they stuck out around us like a broom. The feed sacks were soft cotton and much better than old burlap.) On the bus the girls would talk about what color skirt we would make next. We heated our smoothing iron in front of the fireplace or on the cookstove. We made flour starch so stiff that when we ironed our skirts we could sit them on the floor and they would stand up. When we walked, they would make a crackling noise. We couldn't really sit on the bus well, afraid that we would bend a crease in our skirt.

We had to take our lunch to Horton High—ham biscuits, peanut butter crackers, jelly biscuits. Everyone brought their lunches, as there wasn't a lunchroom in the school. The city students' lunches seemed to be banana sandwiches or other sandwiches with some kind of flat meat in between the bread—maybe bologna. We country students had never eaten that kind of lunch before so we would ask to swap lunches with the city students. I didn't know how good my ham biscuit really was until I got some of their soft, wet bread hung in the roof of my mouth.

After Papa began selling chickens from the hothouse, we had more money. We had two cents a day that we could spend at June Reeves's café, which was down the street from the school. At the café, a Danish was five cents and so was a Royal Crown cola. The colas were so big that we could divide them. They were so good. Sometimes we had a cheese sandwich. We shared all of our food with other children who were standing at the corner of the schoolhouse watching other students eat.

The school later began building a lunchroom. We all talked about saving our money to eat in the lunchroom. Our meals were going to be ten cents each. On the first day that the lunchroom was open, I was asked to help cook with one of the teachers, Miss Lambert, for the other teachers, the principal, whose name was Professor Ben Lee, and the superintendent. (The students didn't eat in the lunchroom that day.) We cooked beef stew, spinach, and for dessert, a lemon pie with meringue. I never knew an egg white would fluff up like that. Before the meringue got stiff my arm became so tired, as I had only two forks to beat it with.

MANY PEOPLE TELL ME how my biscuits are just like their mama's or grandma's or that when they come to the restaurant they find a lot of things that they have not eaten in a long time. They never learned to cook the way their grandma or mama cooked. For those women, and for me, it was all about "dump cooking"—cooking without precise measurements. Dump cooking is for the everyday meal. I would use a sprinkling of salt and pepper and other spices, cooking and tasting to see what the dish needed. With pies and cakes, you have to measure more precisely. However, it makes you feel like more of a cook when you are able to suit your family's taste by experimenting with adding certain spices. And it doesn't take much to make something pretty. Put red or green peppers across a dish, or make a radish rose. Dump cooking is asking Grandma, "How do you cook this?" and she says, "Put a little of this and little of that in." So many people never really taught themselves how to cook. Grandma often is the special cook in their family.

Some of the people who read my first cookbook call it "good history," because they liked my stories about my childhood. Customers at the restaurant also often say that their meal brought back memories about how food was prepared when they were children. Even simple things like using butter in cooked vegetables seems to bring back memories.

During my speaking engagements, someone always asks me who was the most popular person who ever came into Mama Dip's. I always think of Michael Jordan. He used to stop by the restaurant, first when he was a student at UNC and later during his professional basketball years. Still, I tell them that I think "famous people" means anyone who comes through my restaurant door and wants to eat my country cooking. And my kids say that when a customer tries chitlins, it makes them a bona fide customer.

I have received many letters, phone calls, and emails from people who saw the TV shows, bought the cookbook, and cooked the recipes. They often ask questions about ingredients they cannot get in their area. One lady called me from Jamaica and wondered where she could get chicken seasoning packets. Others want to know what self-rising flour is, how it is different from plain flour. They also ask about where they can get smaller chickens. I tell them to ask their grocers to order smaller chickens, because more people are using smaller amounts of chicken. This is surprisingly one of the most common things they call about—the chickens in their grocery store are too big for the recipes.

Some people send me recipes. There are many good cooks, many different ways to prepare food, and many spices and seasonings to cook with.

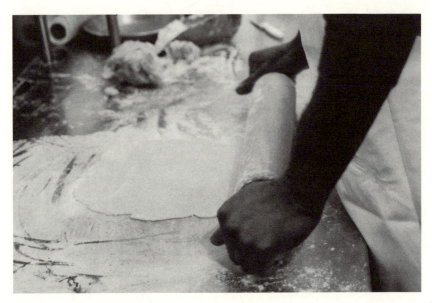

Joe Nathan Council rolling out dough for a piecrust. Photograph by Chelsea Birchfield-Finn.

Sometimes people want to make something that they ate in a restaurant or at a party. I always tell people never to feel bad about asking the waitperson or cook about the seasonings in a dish. I have found that people enjoy eating out and then experimenting at home with new spices that they tasted in the restaurant.

WHEN PEOPLE ASK about my jellies, I tell them that I have been canning, especially making jellies, since I was a little girl. Everything was wild when we were canning in the country. The only time we used "tame" strawberries was for making pies. For jellies, we combed the edge of the pine woods and found blackberries, blueberries, little strawberries, and apples to use. We used the whole apple to make preserves, and the preserves were chunky. Some people have never heard of that. We would find damson plums that ripen in August and September and have a tangy

Annette Council at the cash register in the entrance of the restaurant. Mama Dip's jams, jellies, and chow-chow are displayed on shelves. Photograph by Chelsea Birchfield-Finn.

taste. We had to go from farm to farm looking for a damson tree, and we all shared the fruit when we found one. We used many types of jellies to make bread pudding, but damson plums were the best because they made it so tasty.

We also made our own candy. We put molasses in a pot and cooked it slowly until bubbles formed around the edge. We didn't have a candy thermometer, so we would drop some of the hot molasses into a cup with cold water. If it hardened just as soon as it hit the water and made a ball, the candy was ready.

We always had a pound of store-bought lard for special things like candy and cake filling. We greased a special big platter with the lard and poured the molasses in slowly to cool. Two people would grease their hands so the candy would not stick. Each would take half and work it together until just right. Then they would pull it until it turned real shiny. It would be twisted into a rope and laid on paper. Garlic would sometimes be put in it for our bad colds. Papa would take the handle of a knife and break it into about two-inch pieces. The horehound bush made good molasses candy, too.

We also had molasses candy with peanuts that were roasted in the oven. To roast peanuts the oven had to be cooler than for baking biscuits, so we had to prepare this candy after we got through with supper. The syrup and sugar would be bound together and put in a biscuit pan. Peanuts would be mixed in and when the candy was ready to eat, Papa would break it up with the hammer.

We made molasses popcorn, too. The corn was left on the corncob until ready to be popped. Then we would shell it off with the side of our thumbs. When we had enough, we would have to blow the cob crumbs out of the corn before we popped it, because we didn't want crumbs in our popcorn. We used a fry pan that was not cast-iron—it was made of tin, and it would burn everything if we didn't watch it closely. We would put grease in the pan and pour in the popcorn, then just stand there and shake the pan. Every time a grain would pop we would shake, shake, and shake until there were no more pops. Then we would pick out all the popcorn and put it into the yellow bowl that always held the peas and cabbage and pour butter over it.

Sometimes Roland, a family friend who helped my father around the farm and stayed with us when I was young, would mix Karo syrup with butter for the popcorn. One person would pour the syrup and another would stir the corn. We had to share the jobs of stirring and pouring. Sometimes we would argue about whose turn it was to stir or to pour. Roland would put a spoonful of this buttery syrup on a piece of paper to cool, one for each of us. He told us that we could eat our spoonful now or take it to school. We didn't take it to school but one time, because when we gave everyone there a taste, we only had a little bit left for ourselves. That was one of the best sweet treats we had.

Our chewing gum was sap from the sweet gum tree and the pine tree. Small sweet gum trees grew almost everywhere. The leaves looked like those of the wild cherry tree, but the sweet gum never had blooms or fruit. It turned almost maroon in early fall. We would have to cut a chip out of the tree first. Then, as the tree began to heal, the sap would roll down, and the sweet sap was like chewing gum. We would stick big nails in the sweet gum tree to make holes in it. Then in the spring and summer at our play times, we would race to see how much sap had leaked out. The rosin from the pine would stick to our teeth if it wasn't rock dry. The sweet gum was always special, because the sweet gum tree didn't give out candy sap easily.

Aunt Laura taught us how to make our toothbrushes out of the young sweet gum bush. She told us to stretch out our arms and when we saw a limb about as long as our arms, to break our toothbrush from that limb. We would bend the little limbs toward us, looking for our size. When we found one, we skinned the leaves off and broke off a piece a little longer than our first finger. Next we asked a buddy to cut off the end of the stick with a pocket knife. We would then chew the end, put it in some water, and bite off the long stringy pieces. Aunt Laura would give us baking soda to take home to put by the washstand. We were supposed to dip one end of the toothbrush in the soda and brush up and down on our teeth. When we saw Aunt Laura on Sunday, she would check with us to see if we had brushed our teeth.

Aunt Laura always carried a small box of tuberose snuff in her apron pocket, along with a homemade handkerchief to hold the snuff down. The ladies of the community all dipped snuff. Nowadays, no one seems to dip snuff anymore.

Aunt Laura also made big biscuits we called "cat fish heads." Without a biscuit cutter, she would mash the biscuits flat with her knuckles, and they would always all come out one size. I never quite knew how she got them to be the same size. Papa liked my little biscuits. We never had a biscuit cutter either, but our Aunt Mary did.

I learned to cook on a wood-fired stove, and the temperature was never exact. The pots had to be moved from side to side to simmer slowly. A kettle of water was always kept on the stove so hot water could be added to the pot as needed. We didn't have any fancy cooking gadgets, and I still don't today, just a few good pots and pans, some skillets, a mixing bowl, a spoon, and a potato masher. We seasoned our food by eye and feel and taste, making do with what we had. We liked to try different flavors in our sweet potato pie by adding different spices. We also liked to mix

Pots of vegetables on the stove in the restaurant. Photograph by Tom Finn.

vegetables together, like crowder peas and limas, especially when we had only a little of each. It was very common in country cooking to mix vegetables together. I still do it today.

SOMETIMES I WONDER who I am this late in life, but I am thankful for everything. I am amazed at the recognition that has been given to me. On October 5, 1999, soon after my first cookbook was published, a Kentucky colonel popped up in my doorway and handed me a plaque that announced that I was now a Kentucky colonel, the highest honor given by the governor of Kentucky. When he handed the plaque to me, the first thing I thought about was chicken.

On June 29, 2000, I met the governor of North Carolina, Jim Hunt, and I received a plaque from the Order of the Longleaf Pine, the highest honor that North Carolina gives to its citizens. That was a shock. It was a thrill to me to meet the governor, so when I went I took Governor

Elaine Council, restaurant manager, packing a pie to be shipped to a customer. Photograph by Tom Finn.

Hunt a pecan pie. He couldn't wait until we finished talking so he could cut a piece of pie right away and eat it.

I won the North Carolina Small Business Award in 2002 and went to Washington, D.C., to compete with the winners from the other 50 states and 2 territories for the national award. My daughter Spring went to Washington with me. I won third place in the national competition, and right after the last award was given at the awards ceremony and luncheon, Spring and I and the other winners were whisked off to the White House. There I met the president, his cocker spaniel, and his terrier. It was an exciting time in Washington.

The town of Chapel Hill proclaimed May 16, 2002, as Mildred "Mama Dip" Cotton Council Day. Mayor Kevin Foy presented the award to me at a Chamber of Commerce gathering. The proclamation stated that the award was based on my being an active citizen of our community for nearly my entire life, for my contribution to our community through the church and many other organizations, for being a major employer of indigent or homeless workers, training and coaching them in not only work skills but also life skills, and for the positive attention our community had gained through my restaurant, my first cookbook, and my numerous appearances on national television.

Not long ago, I had another surprise. Rachael Ray is the hostess of a television show called *$40 a Day*, on which she travels to different locations in search of good food. The catch is that she has only $40 a day for dining out. In the summer of 2004 Rachael Ray and her producers came to Mama Dip's Kitchen. Ms. Ray had heard about my catfish gumbo and wanted to try it. (I had made it on UNC TV for a fund-raiser.) First the film crew filmed me making catfish gumbo in the restaurant kitchen, while Ms. Ray ate breakfast at another restaurant in town. She then went to a bookstore, bought my cookbook, and then came to the restaurant for lunch. The crew filmed her coming in and eating the catfish gumbo. It was interesting to watch the filming of this show featuring Chapel Hill and Mama Dip's Kitchen. It was broadcast on the Food Network on August 31 that year.

DURING THIS SUCCESSFUL time in my life, I still felt like myself—the same Mildred Council—and I kept up my work in the community. Community was always important to me when I was growing up. We all helped each other out when needed.

The men in the area had something called a wood frolic, where they went from farm to farm in a group and cut down trees, chopped them up, and stacked wood on each farm for the winter months. We could hear the ax and crosscut saw from far away hacking deep into the trees and the men using the ax to cut big chips out of the trees. With one man on each end of the crosscut saw, they would work together. We could hear music from the saw as it cut through the big logs. The men had fun making bets and daring each other and offering prizes to each other for the fastest sawing. The prize was usually a drink of white liquor. The winner would step around the corner and claim his drink. The axes hit the log, and it would split wide open. We children would keep stacking up the wood, hurrying to see who would make the biggest pile. We were always given a prize at the end, usually a horehound or peppermint stick from town or something from the candy man.

Church was the shrine of our community. When we went to church on Sunday, it felt like we were going to meet the angels. I attended Hamlet Chapel CME church when I was growing up. The elder women of the church always had something special for us, the motherless children. It wasn't always peppermint sticks or molasses candy but instead a lesson about the world around us and how we could grow up to be little giants, like King David, if we wanted. Part of the church community was coming together to have church suppers. We used to have these suppers during the day, but nowadays we seem to have them at night.

Our church would hold an "August meeting," which was an annual homecoming for all who attended the church. We would all gather at the church, and if we had caused trouble or told a lie or done something wrong during the year, the stewards and stewardesses of the church would bring us up to kneel at the altar, which was a symbolic mourning bench. Then everyone would sing and pray until we made our confession. Later, all who had been to the mourning bench had to stand and say their name and be put on the church membership roll. I dreaded the year that I would be 12, because this was when we *had* to go up to the mourning bench and make our confessions in church. When I was eleven I knew it was around the corner for me. I just wanted to cook and feed people, not make my confessions.

I loved the time around Easter and Children's Day. We had to go to the church on Saturdays to practice for Children's Day, which was the second Sunday in June. It was a special day for everyone to show their talent. Usually we walked to the church. We were given two or three pennies to stop by the Petty Store, a little red store by the road just a little out of our way. We would go in and buy a Mary Jane for a penny or a horehound or peppermint stick, eat some, and then run half way to the church. We would pick the candy out of our teeth, catch our breath, and be fresh when we got to church to practice.

I had to give my first recitation speech on Easter Sunday when I was 12. When I walked into church that Sunday I thought to myself, "What y'all looking at me for? I didn't come here to stay. I came here to let you know that this is Easter day." Well, I gave my recitation speech, and just as soon as I crossed my legs and made my bow, I cried so hard I couldn't find my way back to the bench. The women hugged and hugged me, and I sniffed until I sniffed myself to sleep across some lady's lap.

People from Chapel Hill would always visit our house and farm. My sister Bernice, who lived in town, would be tired from working and would pay someone to bring her home to the farm. Everyone would come by the house during the August church meeting weekend, including Miss Lambert, my teacher. She always knew we would be cooking a lot of good food. We had many community events at the church, and I always liked being part of it.

NOWADAYS I ENJOY being on the boards of organizations in the community, particularly human services boards. All the other members of the boards are much, much younger than me, and I can give them insight about the community—where we have come from, what we are facing, and what conditions affect poverty in the community.

I worked with prisons for many years because I felt that when the inmates were released there was a need for them to be accepted back into the community. We volunteers sat down and ate with the prisoners and talked with them about coming back into the community. We talked about their wives and children and what it would take to be back with them. We listened. We had yard sales to buy Christmas presents for their children.

I also like to work with the Department of Aging because I believe that the older generation built America with our bare hands. Now we have technology to do the things that we did with our hands, from digging ditches to working in the kitchen. In our community we call our elderly people "experienced citizens."

Head Start is also one of my favorite community organizations. It has improved the conditions for children in communities all over the United States through early intervention.

Mama Dip, Della Jeffers, and Geary Wayne Council working in the restaurant kitchen. Photograph by Tom Finn.

I like to help fund-raise for other community projects, such as the March of Dimes, which helps so many children get the medical help that they need, and the Ronald McDonald House, which houses the families of children hospitalized with long-term illnesses. I like to help with our public television station, UNC TV, because some of the documentaries that they produce are about slavery, the Revolutionary War, and scientific subjects. They also have a business program that I can look at in the morning, as well as the news. Most of the TV I watch is UNC TV specials. I love the Irish Riverdancers.

I am also involved in an annual community dinner in Chapel Hill. Nerys Levy and I formed a committee seven years ago to improve human relationships through culture, food, dress, and the arts. It doesn't matter whether the people participating each year in the dinner can speak English or not—we all come together at this event. Different restaurants and churches cook, and five to six hundred people attend every year. We have amateur cultural performances, including music and dance. Sometimes a cultural group will do a blessing of the table and food in its own language. This is a very interesting way for any community to get together.

There are so many volunteers for this event. The Girl Scouts pour tea, elderly people from assisted living homes help, and some professors from the universities and a range of public officials help serve. Many different businesses bring in food of all types, including Mexican, Italian, Asian, and so on. We have gospel singing, dance, instrumental music, and a lot of other things for entertainment. In September of 2004, this community event won a North Carolina Restaurant Association Community Involvement Award.

This is our community. We live and work together, we cook, and then we bring food to share—and we share the recipes with each other also. We never forget about our neighbors, our families, our friends.

The old people dream dreams and the young people see visions. I have lived the dream of building up Mama Dip's, and I hope my children will find the vision of how to carry it on.

Cooking and Serving Basics

Utensils in My Kitchen

potato peeler
paring knife
casing knife
French cleaver
sifter
strainer (medium and small)
    with handle
colander (plastic)
hand mixer
nonstick muffin pans
10-inch cast-iron frying pan
6-inch cast-iron frying pan
electric frying pan
2 (9-inch) pie pans
3 (9-inch) layer cake pans
2-quart casserole dish
9 × 13-inch casserole pan
pastry brushes

Staples in My Pantry

flour
cornmeal
grits
oatmeal
rice
spices
sugar
pasta
canned salmon
canned tuna
cream of chicken soup
cream of mushroom soup
evaporated milk
diced tomatoes
tomato paste
tomato sauce
tomato puree
white potatoes
onions
crushed pineapple
Jell-O

Measurements to Remember

3 teaspoons = 1 tablespoon

4 tablespoons = ¼ cup

8 tablespoons = ½ cup

5 tablespoons = ⅓ cup

10 tablespoons + 2 teaspoons = ⅔ cup

12 tablespoons = ¾ cup

16 tablespoons = 1 cup

½ cup + 2 tablespoons = ⅝ cup

4 ounces = ½ cup

8 ounces = 1 cup

1 pound = 2 cups sugar

1 pound = 4 cups sifted flour

1 pound = 2⅔ cup powdered sugar

1 pound = 4 sticks butter or margarine

¼ stick butter or margarine = 2 tablespoons

½ stick butter or margarine = 4 tablespoons or ¼ cup

1 stick butter or margarine = ¼ pound

Setting Up a Buffet Table

I suggest setting up a buffet table for community suppers or for serving meals at home as shown here and on the following page.

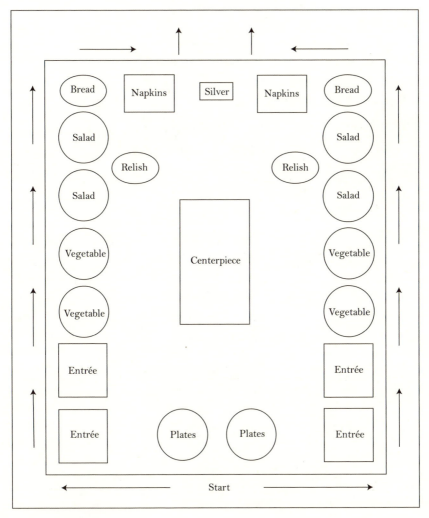

For Community Suppers

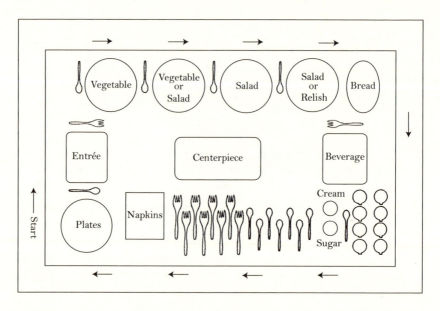

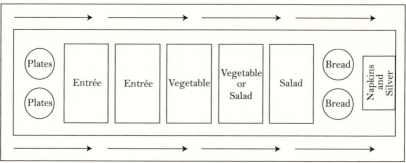

For Home

Breakfast

Grits Casserole

Southern Brunch Shrimp and Grits

Battered Fried Streak of Lean Fatback

Sausage Casserole

Breakfast Pizza

Breakfast Casserole

French Toast

Fried Apple Rings

Grits Casserole

This is good served with fruit and muffins.

4¼ cups water
1 cup yellow grits
1 teaspoon garlic salt
1 pound cheddar cheese, grated
1 stick butter or margarine

4 eggs, beaten
½ cup milk
4 slices bacon, cooked and
 crumbled

Preheat oven to 400°. Put the water in a pot and bring to a boil. Stir in the grits and cook for 4 to 5 minutes until thick, stirring frequently. Add the garlic salt, cheese, and butter and mix well. In a small bowl, beat the eggs together with the milk and add slowly to the grits. Pour the mixture into a greased baking dish and bake for 30 minutes. Remove from the oven and sprinkle bacon over the top. Serve hot.

Serves 8.

Southern Brunch Shrimp and Grits

4¼ cups water
1 cup yellow grits
¼ stick butter or margarine
1 tablespoon lemon juice
2 pounds fresh shrimp, shells on
½ teaspoon garlic salt

½ teaspoon crushed red pepper
6 slices bacon
1 cup chopped white onion
¾ cup flour
1 can (14½ ounces) chicken broth

Put the water in a pot and bring to a boil. Stir in the grits and cook for 4 to 5 minutes until thick, stirring frequently. Add the butter and mix well. Meanwhile, bring another large pot of water to boil and add the lemon juice. Cook the shrimp until pink, about 6 to 8 minutes. Drain the shrimp, peel and devein them, then sprinkle them with the garlic salt and red pepper. Cook the bacon then set it aside, reserving ⅔ cup of the drippings. Cook the onions in the bacon fat about 10 minutes, stirring frequently. Sprinkle the onions with the flour and brown them over medium high heat. Stir the shrimp into the onions and add the broth, if needed. Pour over the grits and crumble the bacon over the top.

Serves 8.

Battered Fried Streak of Lean Fatback

We always thought that this dish was a country breakfast treat. We served it with stewed apples and grits.

½ cup cornmeal
¼ cup flour
12 ½-inch slices streak of lean fatback
vegetable oil for frying

Mix together the cornmeal and flour. Put the meat in a skillet and cover with water. Bring to a boil and cook for 3 minutes to release the salt. Dip the meat into the flour mixture and fry in hot oil until brown on both sides. Drain on paper towels.

Serves 6, 2 slices per person.

Sausage Casserole

2 cups bread crumbs
1 pound bulk sausage, browned
   and drained

1 pound sharp cheese, grated
6 eggs, beaten
2 cups milk

Preheat oven to 350°. In a 9 × 13-inch baking pan, layer the bread crumbs and sausage and top with the cheese. In a small bowl, combine the eggs and milk and pour over the layers in the baking pan. Bake for 30 to 40 minutes until done.

Serves 8.

Breakfast Pizza

1 pound bulk sausage
½ cup chopped onion
½ cup chopped green pepper
1 package (32 ounces) frozen
   hash browns
3 tablespoons milk

6 eggs, beaten
1 package (8 ounces) shredded
   cheddar and Monterey Jack
   cheese
3 tablespoons grated Parmesan
   cheese

Preheat oven to 400°. Brown the sausage in an oven-proof frying pan and drain off most of the fat. Add the onions and peppers and sauté until softened. Spread the hash browns evenly over the sausage mixture. In a small bowl, mix together the milk and eggs and pour over the hash browns. Combine the cheeses and sprinkle over the top. Bake on the lower rack of oven for 10 to 12 minutes until brown.

Serves 6 to 8.

Breakfast Casserole

12 slices French bread
8 eggs, beaten
1 ½ cups milk

¼ cup sugar
½ teaspoon nutmeg
1 teaspoon cinnamon

Topping

1 package (10 ounces) frozen
strawberries, thawed
¼ cup sugar
1 tablespoon cornstarch

2 tablespoons water
10x powdered sugar for
sprinkling (optional)

Butter a 9 × 13-inch baking pan. Lay the bread in a single layer on the bottom of the pan. In a medium bowl, mix the eggs, milk, sugar, nutmeg, and cinnamon. Pour the mixture over the bread. Cover the pan and refrigerate it overnight. When ready to bake, preheat the oven to 450°. Place the baking pan on the oven's middle rack and bake for 20 to 25 minutes.

For the topping, cook the strawberries and sugar in a saucepan over medium heat for about 2 minutes. In a small bowl, combine the cornstarch and water and pour into the strawberries. Cook until the mixture thickens. Sprinkle with the powdered sugar if desired. Serve with maple syrup.

Makes 6 servings, 2 slices each.

French Toast

6 eggs, beaten
1 ¼ cups milk
2 tablespoons sugar
pinch salt

1 teaspoon nutmeg
½ teaspoon cinnamon
12 slices day-old bread
butter for frying

Combine the eggs, milk, sugar, and salt and mix well. Stir in the nutmeg and cinnamon. Dip the bread into the egg mixture to coat both sides. Heat the butter in a large grill or frying pan. Add the bread and brown on both sides. Serve with maple syrup or cooked fresh fruit.

Makes 6 servings, 2 slices each.

Fried Apple Rings

This is country breakfast fare.

3 – 4 firm apples, cored
sugar to taste
½ cup vegetable oil

Cut the apples into ½-inch slices and sprinkle on both sides with the sugar. Heat the oil in a skillet. Add the apples a few at a time and turn them with a spatula until tender and brown.

Serves 6.

Soups and Sandwiches

Cream of Chicken Soup

1 ½ pounds chicken pieces
1 bay leaf
1 can (14½ ounces) chicken broth
3 tablespoons butter
1 cup chopped celery

½ cup chopped onion
3 tablespoons flour
1 small can (5 ounces) evaporated
  milk
salt and black pepper to taste

Wash the chicken, put it in a pot with the bay leaf, and add enough water to cover the meat by about two inches. Bring the water to a boil and cook for 5 minutes. Reduce the heat to medium low, cover the pot, and simmer until the chicken is tender, about 35 minutes. Remove the chicken to cool, reserving the stock; when cool, pull the meat from the bones and chop. Strain the stock and add the canned broth. You will need a good 3 cups of liquid. Add the butter, celery, and onion to a pot and cook over medium heat until the onion is tender but not brown. Stir in the flour, add the broth and evaporated milk, and stir to mix from the bottom. Add the chopped chicken and simmer 5 to 10 minutes. Stir in salt and pepper to taste.

Serves 6.

Turkey Broth

Remove the meat from a roasted turkey, add the bones to a large pot, and cover. Add 6 cups of water with ½ teaspoon poultry seasoning and let come to a rapid boil for 10 minutes. Strain the broth.

Turkey Soup

This soup freezes well.

3 tablespoons vegetable oil
    or margarine
½ cup chopped onion
1 cup chopped celery
1 can (14½ ounces) chicken broth
1 recipe turkey broth (above)

1 cup sliced carrot
½ cup macaroni
4 cups cooked, chopped turkey
parsley, optional
salt and black pepper to taste

Put the oil in a large pot on low heat and add the onion and celery, stirring until the onion is tender but not brown. Add the chicken and turkey broths, stirring well, turn the heat to medium high, and bring to a boil. Lower the heat to medium, add the carrot and macaroni, and cook for 20 minutes. Add the turkey, parsley, salt, and pepper; turn the heat to low and simmer for 30 minutes.

Serves 4.

Corn Chowder

This can be an appetizer or a main dish.

3 slices (3 inches each) salt pork
½ cup chopped sweet onion
3 cups diced potato
3 cups fresh yellow corn, cut from the cob and then the cob scraped
4½ cups milk
1½ teaspoons salt
1 small can (5 ounces) evaporated milk
1 cup chopped lobster, hot (optional)

Cut the salt pork into strips. Wash, put in a pot, and cook, stirring slowly until brown. Remove and set aside, reserving the fat. Stir the onion into the pork fat and cook until tender but not brown, 3 to 4 minutes. Put the potatoes in hot water and boil until tender; drain. Stir in the corn, milk, salt, evaporated milk, and pork pieces and heat on low. Stir in the lobster. Serve with crackers.

Serves 6.

Squash Soup

½ stick butter
¼ tablespoon chopped sweet onion
2 pounds small summer squash, sliced thin
1 large can (12 ounces) evaporated milk
2 cans (14½ ounces each) chicken broth
1 teaspoon garlic salt

Put the butter in a skillet on medium heat and add the onion. When hot, add the squash and stir to mix. Reduce the heat to low and cover the skillet. Let simmer about 15 minutes then mash the softened squash and onion with a potato masher. Stir in the evaporated milk, broth, and garlic salt. Stir while heating the soup to just under the boiling point. Remove from the heat prior to boiling.

Serves 6.

Mama Dip's Catfish Gumbo

¼ teaspoon black pepper
2 teaspoons garlic salt
¼ teaspoon crushed red pepper
2 teaspoons Cajun seasoning
1 bay leaf
¼ cup vegetable oil
1 cup diced onion
1 large green pepper, diced
1 cup sliced celery
3 tablespoons flour

2 cans (14½ ounces each) chicken broth
1 large can (28 ounces) diced tomatoes
1 package (10 ounces) frozen cut okra
1 can (6 ounces) tomato paste
few drops hot sauce
1½ pounds catfish, cut into chunks

Combine the black pepper, garlic salt, crushed red pepper, Cajun seasoning, and bay leaf; set aside. In a large pot over medium heat, add the oil, onion, green pepper, and celery. Stir to coat. Add the flour and stir until blended. Add the chicken broth and stir until smooth. Add the tomatoes, okra, and tomato paste. Stir to mix well. Add the hot sauce and seasonings. Stir to mix. Let the gumbo come to a boil, reduce the heat to low, and let simmer uncovered for 30 minutes. Add the catfish and stir to mix. Cover and let simmer for 20 minutes. Serve with rice.

Serves 6 to 8.

Oyster Stew

1 large can (12 ounces) evaporated milk

2 cups whole milk

2 tablespoons cornstarch

¼ cup water

½ stick butter

1 pint oysters, chopped and sautéed in butter for 8 to 10 minutes

½ teaspoon seasoning salt

½ teaspoon black pepper

Put the evaporated milk and milk in a pot and heat. Do not boil. Mix the cornstarch with the water and add to the pot. Reduce the heat to medium. In a separate pan, heat the butter and add the oysters with their cooking liquid. Simmer for 10 minutes, cooking until the edges of the oysters become curly. Add the oysters and liquid to the hot milk and stir in the salt and pepper. Let simmer for 10 minutes.

Serves 6.

Clam Chowder

I suggest buying sliced salt pork and cutting it into small pieces with scissors.

½ cup lean salt pork (streak of lean), sliced into small pieces

½ cup chopped onion

2 cups finely chopped potato

½ cup water

3½ cups milk

1 large can (12 ounces) evaporated milk

4 cans (6½ ounces each) minced clams, drained

salt and black pepper to taste

Wash the salt pork, put it in a large pot (2½ to 3 quarts), and brown it over low heat. Remove the cooked salt pork from the pot and set aside. Add the onion to the fat in the pot and cook until tender but not brown, 3 to 5 minutes. Stir in the potato, water, milk, and evaporated milk and heat the mixture until hot. Add the clams, reduce the heat to low, and cover the pot. Cook for about 15 minutes until the potato is tender. Stir from the bottom and simmer for 20 minutes. Add salt and pepper to taste. Stir in the salt pork.

Serves 5 to 6.

Haw River Fish Stew

When I was growing up in Chatham County, North Carolina, we used to fish in the Haw River and its branches. Whatever we caught—eel, catfish, bream, or carp—we put in this stew. The carp is not a tasty fish. The only place we would use it was in this stew.

1½ pounds perch, thawed if frozen
2 tablespoons butter or margarine
½ cup chopped onion
3 cups thinly sliced potatoes
2 tablespoons flour

2 cans (14½ ounces each) stewed tomatoes
1 teaspoon crushed red pepper
2 teaspoons seasoning salt

Sauté the fish in the butter, stirring until hot. Add the onion and cook for 3 minutes. Stir in the potatoes and cook until hot. Mix in the flour and then add the tomatoes. Stir from the bottom and add the red pepper and salt. Reduce the heat to low and let simmer for 15 minutes until the potato is tender.

Serves 6.

Roast Beef Hoagie

½ stick butter or margarine
1 teaspoon garlic salt
1 large sweet onion, sliced thin
1 pound thinly sliced roast beef

1 package (8 ounces) shredded
    mozzarella cheese
4 6-inch hoagie buns

Preheat oven to broil. Melt the butter in a frying pan and sprinkle in the garlic salt. Sauté the onion until tender but not brown. Add the roast beef and turn until hot. Spread your preferred amount of cheese over each bun. Broil the buns on the lower rack of the oven until the cheese melts. Remove the buns from the oven and spoon the roast beef mixture onto them.

Makes 4 hoagies.

BLT Sandwich

This old-fashioned sandwich is a real classic.

8 slices bread, toasted
mayonnaise
crisp lettuce

8 thin slices tomato
salt and black pepper
12 slices bacon, fried until crisp

Spread each slice of toast with the mayonnaise, layer with the lettuce and tomato, and sprinkle with salt and pepper. Add the bacon, cut the sandwiches into triangles, and serve.

Makes 4 sandwiches.

Manuel's Mexican Hot Toasted Sandwich

Manuel was an employee at Mama Dip's Kitchen restaurant.

5 eggs, beaten
½ teaspoon salt
½ pound or 16 slices
   mozzarella cheese

16 slices white bread
vegetable oil for frying
sliced jalapeño peppers
   (optional)

Mix the eggs with the salt. Put one slice of cheese on each piece of bread and add peppers. Dip both sides into the egg mixture. Fry until brown on both sides. Cheese should be melted.

Makes 16 open-faced sandwiches.

Pigs in the Blanket

This was a Friday lunch special at the Sigma Chi fraternity on UNC's campus.

8 franks
4 ounces grated cheese
8 slices bacon

Preheat oven to 350°. Split the franks lengthwise and press cheese into the middles. Wrap the bacon slices around the franks, using toothpicks to hold the bacon in place. Place on a baking pan and cook for 20 minutes until hot. Serve with baked beans.

Makes 8.

Salads

Tossed Salad

Layered Spinach-Lettuce Salad

Luncheon Salad Plate

Egg Salad

Egg and Seafood Salad

Shrimp Salad

Salmon Salad

Macaroni and Cheese Salad

Corn Salad

Bean and Corn Salad

Bean Salad

Cabbage Salad

Cucumber Coleslaw

Pickled Okra

Broccoli and Raisin Salad

Carrot Salad

Fruit Jell-O Salad

Tomato Aspic

Orange-Pineapple Salad

Pineapple Salad

Fruit Delight

Fresh Fruit Salad

Cranberry Salad

Ambrosia

Spiced Peaches

Pickled Pineapple

Tossed Salad

1 large head romaine lettuce
3 thin slices small purple or
    sweet onion
1 Granny Smith apple

½ pound tender spinach leaves
¾ cup shredded Parmesan cheese
4–6 slices cooked bacon, crumbled

Cut off about 3 inches from the top of the lettuce and tear it into bite-sized pieces. Wash the lettuce and place it on a paper towel to dry. Separate the sliced onion into rounds. Peel and core the apple, cutting it into quarters and slicing thin. Place the apple pieces in a bowl of cold water with a little salt to keep their color. Toss the lettuce, spinach, and onions together in a bowl. Drain the apples and toss with the lettuce mixture. Add your favorite dressing. Shake the cheese and bacon over each serving.

Serves 6 to 8.

Layered Spinach–Lettuce Salad

½ pound fresh spinach, shredded
1 head lettuce, shredded
¼ cup chopped celery
1 small can (8½ ounces) green peas
10 green onions, chopped
3 hard-boiled eggs, sliced

½ pound baked ham, shredded
1 cup salad dressing mayonnaise
½ cup sour cream
1 tablespoon dry buttermilk
    dressing mix
¼ cup shredded Parmesan cheese

Put the spinach and lettuce in the bottom of a large glass salad bowl. Layer the vegetables, eggs, and ham in order on top of the salad greens. Combine the next 3 ingredients and mix well. Spread this mixture over the top of the salad and sprinkle the Parmesan cheese over the top to the edge of the bowl. Cover tightly and refrigerate for several hours or overnight.

Serves 6 to 8.

Luncheon Salad Plate

1 head lettuce, chopped
6 leaves romaine lettuce,
 sliced into 1-inch pieces
1 medium cucumber, sliced thin
3 small tomatoes, sliced

½ cup thinly sliced radishes
1 small can low-sodium Spam,
 sliced thin
¾ cup crumbled feta cheese

Put the cut lettuce in a bowl and refrigerate to crisp, 3 to 4 hours or overnight. Add the cucumber, tomatoes, and radishes and mix lightly. Toss together with the Spam and cheese. Serve with your favorite vinaigrette dressing.

Serves 6.

Egg Salad

This is good to make for sandwiches or to go on a cold salad plate.

8 large hard-boiled eggs
½ cup sweet pickle relish
1 teaspoon mustard
½ cup mayonnaise

½ teaspoon salt
½ teaspoon black pepper
few drops hot sauce, optional

Grate the eggs into a bowl. Add all of the other ingredients and mix gently. Taste for seasoning.

Serves 8.

Egg and Seafood Salad

6 hard-boiled eggs, chopped
⅔ cup sweet salad cubes
¼ cup crushed saltine crackers
½ cup chopped green pepper

2 tablespoons chopped sweet onion
½ cup mayonnaise
1 pound imitation crabmeat
2 tablespoons black olives, sliced

Mix all the ingredients together and chill. Serve on lettuce.

Serves 6.

Shrimp Salad

4 cups water
1 teaspoon salt
1 tablespoon lemon juice
1½ pounds medium shrimp,
    shells on
1 box (16 ounces) macaroni,
    cooked as directed

½ cup chopped celery
3 hard-boiled eggs, grated
1 small can (8½ ounces) green peas
2 teaspoons horseradish
½ cup mayonnaise
salt to taste

Bring the water to a boil and add the salt, lemon juice, and shrimp.
Boil the shrimp until it turns pink, approximately 6 to 8 minutes.
Drain shrimp and let stand until cool, then peel and devein. Stir in the
remaining ingredients and refrigerate until ready to serve.

Serves 6.

Salmon Salad

1 can (14¾ ounces) red salmon
½ cup sweet salad cubes
3 hard-boiled eggs, grated
½ teaspoon dill

2 teaspoons lemon juice
½ cup mayonnaise
1 tablespoon sliced spring onion,
white part only

Drain the salmon and remove the bones and dark skin. Put in a bowl with the other ingredients and mix together well. Serve on a bed of lettuce or in a sandwich.

Serves 6.

Macaroni and Cheese Salad

2 cups uncooked macaroni,
prepared as directed
1 cup sweet salad cubes
½ cup chopped green pepper

¾ cup mayonnaise
1 cup grated sharp cheese
1 cup grated pepper jack cheese
salt to taste

Mix all the ingredients together and chill.

Serves 6.

Corn Salad

2 cans (15¼ ounces each) yellow
   or white corn, drained
½ cup chopped red bell pepper
½ cup vegetable oil

½ cup vinegar
3 tablespoons sugar
½ teaspoon garlic salt

Mix all the ingredients together in a bowl; refrigerate for 1 hour
before serving.

Serves 6.

Bean and Corn Salad

½ cup cider vinegar
¼ cup oil
2 tablespoons sugar
½ cup ketchup
1 tablespoon lemon juice
1 teaspoon garlic salt, divided
1 can (15 ounces) great northern
   beans

1 can (15 ounces) black beans
1 can (15 ounces) pinto beans
1 can (15¼ ounces) yellow corn,
   drained
1 large cucumber, chopped
3 spring onions, white part only,
   sliced thin

Mix together the first five ingredients and ½ teaspoon of the garlic
salt to make a French dressing. Set aside. In a colander, rinse all of
the beans under cold running water; drain them and pour into a large
bowl. Add the corn, cucumber, onions, and the remaining ½ teaspoon
garlic salt and refrigerate for 1 hour. Drain off any excess liquid
and stir in the French dressing, coating the beans and vegetables.
Refrigerate until ready to serve.

Serves 8.

Bean Salad

This is good for tailgating parties.

1 can (15 ounces) kidney beans, rinsed and drained

1 can (15 ounces) pinto beans, rinsed and drained

1 can (15 ounces) white beans, rinsed and drained

1 can (14½ ounces) cut green beans, rinsed and drained

3 tablespoons diced celery

½ cup chopped green pepper

3 tablespoons chopped onion

1 cup apple cider vinegar

¼ teaspoon garlic salt

¼ cup brown sugar

½ cup salad oil

Toss together the beans, celery, pepper, and onion. Put the vinegar, garlic salt, brown sugar, and salad oil in a saucepan and bring slowly to a boil, stirring until sugar dissolves. Pour at once over the bean mixture. Refrigerate for several hours before serving.

Serves 10.

Cabbage Salad

1 medium cabbage, grated or shredded

½ cup mayonnaise

2 teaspoons sugar

3 tablespoons vinegar

1 teaspoon celery seed

pinch of salt

Mix together all the ingredients. Check for taste. Let stand for 20 minutes, then cover and refrigerate.

Serves 6.

Cucumber Coleslaw

4 cups shredded cabbage
4 cups diced cucumber
1 teaspoon sugar
½ teaspoon salt

½ teaspoon celery seed
1 tablespoon vinegar
½ cup mayonnaise

Toss together the cabbage and cucumber. Sprinkle the sugar, salt, and celery seed over the cabbage mixture and add the vinegar and mayonnaise. Mix together well.

Serves 6

Pickled Okra

1 ½ pounds fresh, tender okra,
   stems trimmed off
8 cloves garlic (1 clove per jar)
8 teaspoons dill seed
   (1 teaspoon per jar)

1 quart white vinegar
½ cup salt
1 ¼ cups water
2 heaping tablespoons
   pickling spice

Pack the okra firmly with a garlic clove and 1 teaspoon of the dill seed into sterilized pint jars and set aside. Bring the vinegar, salt, water, and pickling spice to a boil; reduce heat and simmer for 5 minutes. Strain the vinegar mixture to remove the pickling spice and then pour the hot mixture over the okra, sealing the jars immediately. Place a dish towel in the bottom of a large pot and fill it halfway with hot water. Place the jars of okra inside the pot, processing them in this hot water bath for 5 to 10 minutes.

Makes around 8 pints.

Broccoli and Raisin Salad

2 bunches broccoli, washed and
   cut into pieces
1 bunch spring onions, sliced,
   with a little of the green
1 cup raisins

1 cup coarsely chopped walnuts
1 ½ cups mayonnaise
3 tablespoons vinegar
½ cup sugar
pinch of salt

Mix together the first four ingredients in a large bowl and set aside. In a small bowl, combine the mayonnaise, vinegar, sugar, and salt. Blend well and pour over the broccoli mixture, stirring to coat.

Serves 8.

Carrot Salad

I like to use colored marshmallows for this dish.

2 cups grated carrots
1 cup crushed pineapple, drained
2 cups miniature marshmallows
¼ cup frozen grated coconut,
   thawed

1 ½ cups Cool Whip
½ cup mayonnaise

Put all the ingredients in a bowl and fold to mix. Serve on lettuce.

Serves 6.

Fruit Jell-O Salad

Jell-O was the center of nutrition in food service on the UNC campus in the forties, and in the sixties it was the beauty of the table.

2 small boxes strawberry Jell-O
2 cups boiling water
2 packages (10 ounces each) frozen
   strawberries, thawed and drained

1 pint strawberry yogurt
1 small can (8 ounces) crushed
   pineapple
2 ripe bananas, mashed

Dissolve the Jell-O in hot water and add the strawberries. Add the yogurt, pineapple, and bananas, stirring to mix. Pour into a 2-quart mold and refrigerate until firm. Remove from the mold and serve on lettuce or in a bowl.

Serves 8.

Tomato Aspic

2 cups tomato juice
1 small box lemon Jell-O
½ cup chopped celery
1 small can (8½ ounces) green
   peas, drained

2 tablespoons chopped pimentos,
   drained
2 tablespoons sliced spring onion,
   white part only
chopped green olives (optional)

Put the tomato juice in a pot and bring to a boil. Remove the pot from the stove and stir in the Jell-O until fully dissolved. Refrigerate until just thickened. Add the vegetables, pour the mixture into a mold, and refrigerate until well set.

Serves 6.

Orange-Pineapple Salad

1 small box orange Jell-O
1 cup boiling water
1 small can (8 ounces) crushed
   pineapple, drained

½ cup grated coconut
¼ cup pecans, chopped
whipped topping

In a bowl, dissolve the gelatin in the hot water. Stir in the remaining ingredients. Pour into a 1-quart mold. Refrigerate until set. Serve with whipped topping.

Serves 6.

Pineapple Salad

1 small box lime Jell-O
1 cup hot water
1 small can (8 ounces) crushed
   pineapple, with juice

1 small container (8 ounces)
   sour cream

In a bowl, dissolve the gelatin in the hot water. Add the juice from the pineapple and refrigerate until slightly thickened. Add the sour cream and mix until creamy, then stir in the pineapple. Pour into a mold and refrigerate until firm.

Serves 6.

Fruit Delight

1 large can (15 ounces) mandarin
   oranges, drained
1 small can (8 ounces) crushed
   pineapple, drained
1½ cups miniature marshmallows
1 small container (8 ounces)
   cottage cheese

1 container (8 ounces) Cool Whip
1 small box orange Jell-O,
   prepared as directed
1 cup pecan pieces
1 cup grated coconut

Mix together the fruit and marshmallows. Stir in the cottage cheese and Cool Whip. Add the gelatin and stir to mix. Stir in the pecans. Pour into a 9 × 12-inch casserole dish and sprinkle the coconut over the top.

Serves 6 to 8.

Fresh Fruit Salad

This was part of our family's holiday brunch. Before making this, let the fruit ripen on the counter for 2 to 3 days to get rich with flavor.

1 red grapefruit, peeled and cut
   into sections
2 cups cantaloupe, peeled and cut
   into chunks
1 mango, peeled and cut into
   chunks
1 large can (15¼ ounces) pineapple
   chunks, drained

1 cup seedless grapes, split
1 small can (11 ounces) mandarin
   oranges, drained
1 cup peaches, peeled and diced
2 teaspoons corn syrup
1 teaspoon lemon juice

Put all the ingredients in a large serving bowl and mix gently to combine.

Serves 8.

Cranberry Salad

½ cup orange juice
2 pounds fresh cranberries
½ cup brown sugar
2 small boxes orange Jell-O
1 cup boiling water

1 cup diced celery
1 small can (11 ounces) mandarin
   oranges, drained
1 cup macadamia nuts, chopped

Add the orange juice, cranberries, and brown sugar to a saucepan and cook over medium heat, stirring until the cranberries burst. Set aside to cool. Dissolve the Jell-O in the boiling water. Stir in the cranberry mixture, celery, oranges, and nuts. Pour into a pan and chill overnight. Cut into squares.

Serves 8.

Ambrosia

This is a Christmastime treat that can be served before the main meal.

2 tablespoons orange juice
2 grapefruits, peeled and cut
   into sections
2 large oranges, peeled and cut
   into sections
1 Red Delicious apple, chopped

1 cup seedless grapes (allow to
   ripen on counter for 2 to 3 days)
1 package (6 ounces) frozen
   grated coconut
2 tablespoons powered sugar
   or to taste

Pour the orange juice over the remaining ingredients, mix gently, and chill.

Serves 6.

Spiced Peaches

These peaches keep well. They can be used as a side dish at a regular meal or at a brunch.

½ cup vinegar
½ cup sugar
3 3-inch cinnamon sticks
1 teaspoon whole cloves

1 teaspoon allspice
2 cans (15 ½ ounces each) peach
    halves, drained

Put the vinegar, sugar, and spices into a saucepan and mix well; simmer over low heat for about 5 minutes. Put the peaches in a bowl, pour the spice mixture over them, and stir to mix. Cover and let ripen in the refrigerator overnight.

Serves 8.

Pickled Pineapple

1 fresh pineapple
¼ cup brown sugar
¼ cup vinegar
1 cup water

1 teaspoon whole cloves
1 tablespoon lemon juice
2 cinnamon sticks

Allow the pineapple to ripen on a counter. When ripe, peel the fruit and cut into chunks or slices. Add the sugar, vinegar, water, cloves, lemon juice, and cinnamon sticks to a pot and bring to a boil. Pour the hot liquid over the pineapple pieces then put in a tightly covered container and refrigerate overnight.

Serves 8.

Breads

1950s Community Biscuit Mix

Country-Style Biscuits

Cheese Biscuits

Herb Biscuits

Chicken Biscuits

Angel Cinnamon-Raisin Biscuits

Cranberry-Sweet Potato-Nut Bread

Cranberry-Nut Bread

Green Tomato Bread

Sweet Potato Muffins

Pumpkin Muffins

Blueberry-Lemon Muffins

Peach Muffins

Hot Water Cornbread

Cheese Cornbread

Cornmeal Patties

Spoon Bread

Pone Bread

Breakfast Hoecake

1950s Community Biscuit Mix

After we moved from Chatham County to Orange County, the county nurse
taught many how to cook with powdered milk. I wondered how they used it.
When powdered milk came to the markets my children were small, and the
community health nurse kept a check on all children making sure that they got
milk in their diets. We used dried milk to make bread and other dishes.

1 gallon all-purpose flour
½ cup baking powder
1 tablespoon salt

2 cups powdered milk
1¾ cups shortening
water or milk

In a bowl, mix all the dry ingredients, then blend in the shortening
with your fingertips until it disappears and the mixture looks like
cornmeal. Put the mixture in a covered jar and store in the cabinet;
do not refrigerate. To make 10 to 12 biscuits, preheat over to 400°.
Mix together 2 cups of the flour mixture and about ¾ cup water or
milk. Roll the dough out on a floured board to about ½-inch thickness.
Cut out the biscuits and place them on a greased baking pan. Bake for
10 to 12 minutes.

Country-Style Biscuits

3 cups all-purpose flour
½ teaspoon salt
4 teaspoons baking powder

¾ cup lard
1 cup buttermilk

Preheat oven to 400°. In a bowl, mix the flour, salt, and baking powder.
Blend in the lard with your fingertips or a fork. Work in the buttermilk
enough to make a soft dough. Knead the dough on a floured countertop
and pinch into 12 pieces. Place the pieces on a greased baking sheet
then roll and flatten them with your knuckles. Bake for 15 minutes.

Makes 12.

Cheese Biscuits

1 package (8 ounces) grated
   sharp cheese
1 stick butter or margarine

2 cups self-rising flour
1 teaspoon baking powder

Preheat oven to 400°. In a large bowl, combine the cheese and butter.
In another bowl, combine the flour and baking powder then add to the
cheese mixture, mixing together like biscuit dough. Turn the dough
out onto floured wax paper and roll out to about ¼-inch thickness. Cut
the biscuits out with a small cutter and place on a greased baking pan.
Bake for 10–12 minutes or until light brown.

Makes 15 to 20.

Herb Biscuits

These biscuits are also good reheated.

3 cups self-rising flour
1 teaspoon dried thyme
2 teaspoons ranch dressing mix

1 teaspoon baking powder
¾ cup shortening
1¼ cups buttermilk

Preheat oven to 400°. In a bowl, mix the flour, thyme, ranch dressing
mix, and baking powder. Blend in the shortening with a fork or your
fingertips and add the buttermilk. Place the dough on a floured board
and knead until the mixture comes together. Roll out the dough to
½-inch thickness. Cut the biscuits out with a 1 ½- or 2-inch cutter
and bake on a greased baking sheet for 15 minutes. Brush with butter
and serve hot.

Makes 12.

Chicken Biscuits

2 ½ cups all-purpose flour
¼ teaspoon baking powder
¼ teaspoon poultry seasoning

½ stick cold butter
½ stick cold margarine
1 cup chicken broth

Preheat oven to 450°. Sift together the flour, baking powder, and poultry seasoning. Blend in the butter and margarine with a fork or your fingertips, then mix in the broth to make a dough. Put the dough on a lightly floured board and knead to make a ball. Press down the ball and then roll the dough to ½-inch thickness. Cut the biscuits out, dipping the biscuit cutter in flour to keep it from sticking to the dough. Place the biscuits on a greased baking sheet and bake for 12 to 15 minutes.

Makes 10 to 12.

Angel Cinnamon-Raisin Biscuits

1 package yeast
2 tablespoons lukewarm water
2 cups self-rising flour
¼ cup sugar
1 teaspoon baking powder
1 tablespoon cinnamon

1 teaspoon salt
½ cup raisins
½ cup shortening
2 cups buttermilk, brought
    to room temperature

Preheat oven to 400°. In a small bowl, dissolve the yeast in the water
and set aside. In a large bowl, combine the flour, sugar, baking powder,
cinnamon, salt, and raisins. Mix the shortening into the flour mixture
and set aside. Add the dissolved yeast to the buttermilk and mix well.
Turn the dough out onto a floured board or countertop and knead
together well. Pinch the dough into 12 pieces and place on a greased
baking sheet, rolling and flattening each piece with your knuckles.
Bake for 15 to 20 minutes.

Makes 12.

Cranberry-Sweet Potato-Nut Bread

3 cups self-rising flour
½ teaspoon ginger
1 teaspoon cinnamon
1 teaspoon baking soda
½ cup sugar
¼ cup brown sugar, packed
1 can (16 ounces) mashed sweet
   potatoes

2 large eggs
1 cup vegetable oil
½ cup orange juice
1 cup dried cranberries,
   cut in half
¾ cup chopped pecans

Preheat oven to 350°. Mix the flour, spices, and baking soda in a large bowl and set aside. In another bowl, mash the sugar, brown sugar, and sweet potatoes until well blended. Add the eggs, oil, and juice until mixed well. Add to the flour mixture and stir just until combined. Stir in the cranberries and pecans. Pour into 2 greased 5 × 9-inch pans and bake for 50 minutes. Let sit in the pan 12 to 15 minutes before removing and then place on a rack to cool.

Makes 2 loaves, 18 1-inch slices.

Cranberry-Nut Bread

1 cup cranberries, cut in half
¾ cup orange juice
1 cup brown sugar, packed
¼ cup vegetable oil

2 cups self-rising flour
½ teaspoon baking soda
1 egg, beaten
½ cup chopped pecans (optional)

Preheat oven to 350°. In a saucepan, mix together the cranberries, orange juice, and brown sugar. Cook over medium heat 8 to 10 minutes until very hot. Add the oil, remove the pan from the heat, and let cool. Sift the flour with the baking soda into a bowl. Stir in the cranberry mixture and the egg. Add the pecans. Pour into a well-greased 5 × 9-inch loaf pan and bake for 50 minutes.

Makes 1 loaf, 9 1-inch slices.

Green Tomato Bread

After eating in my restaurant or cooking from my cookbook, many people send me their own recipes. This recipe was one of those mailed to me.

3 eggs, beaten
1 cup sugar
1 cup vegetable oil
1 teaspoon salt
1 teaspoon vanilla extract
1 cup grated green tomato,
   drained

1 ½ cups all-purpose flour
½ teaspoon baking soda
1 cup chopped nuts
1 cup raisins, optional

Preheat oven to 350°. To the eggs, add the sugar, oil, salt, vanilla, and tomato. Blend in the flour, baking soda, nuts, and raisins. Pour the batter into 2 greased and floured loaf pans and bake for 1 hour.

Makes 1 loaf, 9 1-inch slices.

Sweet Potato Muffins

¾ cup self-rising flour
1 teaspoon baking powder
3 tablespoons brown sugar
½ cup chopped pecans
1 egg, beaten

¼ cup milk
1 cup cold, mashed sweet potatoes
   (you may use canned yams)
3 tablespoons vegetable oil

Preheat oven to 375°. Combine the flour, baking powder, brown sugar, and nuts in a large bowl. In another bowl, mix the eggs, milk, and sweet potatoes; add the oil, stirring until smooth. Add to the flour mixture and stir just until mixed. Spoon the batter into a greased muffin pan and bake for 25 minutes.

Makes 8 to 12.

Pumpkin Muffins

1 box yellow cake mix
1 tablespoon self-rising flour
1 can (15 ounces) pumpkin
2 eggs, beaten

½ cup milk
½ teaspoon cinnamon
½ teaspoon allspice
½ cup chopped pecans (optional)

Preheat oven to 375°. Mix all the ingredients together until well blended. Grease 2 muffin pans or line them with paper baking cups and spoon in the batter. Bake for 30 minutes; when done, muffins should feel solid.

Makes 2 dozen.

Blueberry-Lemon Muffins

2 ½ cups self-rising flour
1 teaspoon baking soda
1 small box lemon pudding mix
½ cup sugar

3 tablespoons butter, melted
2 eggs, beaten
2 cups buttermilk
1 cup blueberries

Preheat oven to 400°. In a bowl, combine the flour, baking soda, pudding mix, and sugar. In another bowl, mix the butter, eggs, and buttermilk. Stir into the flour mixture just until mixed; stir in the blueberries. Spoon by ¼ cups into well-greased or paper-lined muffin pan. Bake for 15 to 20 minutes until brown.

Makes 12.

Peach Muffins

2 cups self-rising flour
¼ teaspoon baking soda
3 tablespoons sugar
1 egg, beaten
2 tablespoons vegetable oil

1 ½–2 cups milk
2 cups chopped ripe peaches
1 teaspoon cinnamon
cinnamon sugar (optional)

Preheat oven to 425°. Mix together the flour, baking soda, sugar, egg, oil, and milk. Combine the peaches with the cinnamon and fold into the batter. Fill muffin cups three-quarters full and bake for 20 to 25 minutes. Sprinkle with cinnamon sugar, if desired.

Makes 12.

Hot Water Cornbread

2 cups cornmeal
1 teaspoon sugar
1 cup boiling water
vegetable oil for frying

Mix all the ingredients. Heat the oil over medium heat in a 10-inch frying pan. Drop two tablespoons of the batter into the hot oil for each patty and then fry until brown on both sides. To make a hoecake instead of patties, spread the batter over the whole skillet and brown on both sides.

Serves 6 to 8.

Cheese Cornbread

1 cup self-rising cornmeal
1 cup cream-style corn
2 large eggs, beaten
1 cup buttermilk

¼ stick butter or margarine
2 teaspoons finely chopped
   hot chili peppers
1 cup shredded cheddar cheese

Preheat oven to 350°. In a bowl, stir together the cornmeal and corn. Add the eggs, buttermilk, butter, and peppers and stir to mix, then add the cheese. Pour the batter into a greased 10-inch cast-iron pan. Bake for 40 minutes or until done.

Serves 6 to 8.

Cornmeal Patties

¼ cup vegetable oil
1 cup self-rising cornmeal
1 egg
milk

Heat the oil in a frying pan. Mix the cornmeal with the egg and enough milk to make a pancake batter–like consistency. Drop 2 tablespoons of the batter into the hot oil for each patty and then fry on both sides until brown and crispy. Drain the cooked patties on paper towels. To serve, top each patty with some cooked Swiss chard, broth, or molasses with butter.

Makes about 6.

Spoon Bread

1 cup self-rising cornmeal
2 teaspoons sugar
pinch baking soda
1 teaspoon salt

1 cup boiling water
1½ cups buttermilk
3 eggs
¼ stick butter, melted

Preheat oven to 375°. Put the cornmeal in a bowl and add the sugar, baking soda, and salt. Stir in the boiling water. Add the buttermilk and then the eggs and butter and mix together well. Pour the batter into a greased cast-iron skillet and bake for 30 minutes.

Serves 6 to 8.

Pone Bread

This is good with cooked fresh greens or fresh fried fish.

5 cups white or yellow cornmeal
3 tablespoons molasses
2 tablespoons shortening or oil
4 cups very hot water

6 tablespoons sugar
1 cup cold water
1 teaspoon salt

Preheat oven to 350°. In a bowl, mix the cornmeal, molasses, and shortening. Stir in the hot water. Add the sugar, cold water, and salt and mix well. Cover and refrigerate the dough for 4 to 6 hours or overnight. Pour into a greased 9 × 12-inch baking pan or dish and bake at 350° for 1 hour; reduce the heat to 300°, cover the pan, and bake for 1 hour and 25 minutes. Let cool and cut into squares to serve.

Serves 8.

Breakfast Hoecake

It was a family tradition to pass the bread around, with each person breaking off a piece for him- or herself before passing it on.

½ cup evaporated milk
½ cup chicken broth
2½ cups self-rising flour

1 teaspoon baking powder
¾ stick cold butter or margarine

Preheat oven to 400°. In a bowl, stir together the milk and broth and set aside. In another bowl, mix together the flour and baking powder. Cut the butter into pieces and then mix them into the flour until the mixture is crumbly. Blend in the liquid ingredients. Turn the dough out onto a floured board and knead it together. Pat the dough evenly into a greased 9 × 13-inch baking pan and bake for 15 minutes until brown.

Serves 6.

Meat, Poultry, and Seafood

Pork Roast with Yams

Stuffed Boneless Pork Loin

Pork Casserole

Oven-Barbecued Baby Back Ribs

Souse Meat

Sausage and Green Pepper Skillet Supper

Baked Beans, Franks, and Cheese Casserole

Cornmeal Gravy

Beef Roasted in a Bag

Chuck Roast

Old-Fashioned Corned Beef Hash

Country-Style Hamburger Steak

Meat Loaf

Meat Loaf with Horseradish
  and Mushrooms

Meat Loaf in a Blanket

Brown Beef Gravy

Hamburger Goulash

Shepherd's Pie

Beef-o-Roni

Porcupine Meatballs

Hamburger, Macaroni,
    and Cheese Casserole

Spaghetti Sauce

Lasagna

Spinach Lasagna

Breaded Veal Cutlets

Roasted Chicken

Roast Capon with Dressing

Capon Gravy

Baked Hen

Braised Chicken

Chicken Tetrazzini

Chicken Tortilla Stew

Honey Mustard Chicken Breast

Marinated Drumsticks

Fruity Chicken

Spicy Hot Chicken Thighs

Creole Chicken Thighs

Country-Style Smothered
  Chicken Gizzards

Turkey à la King

Chicken Noodle Pie

Chicken Croquettes

Chicken Noodle Casserole

Chicken Noodle Casserole with
  Tortilla Crust

Turkey Noodle Casserole

Barbecue Turkey Franks

Giblet Gravy

Crab Cakes I

Crab Cakes II

Country Fish Cakes

Sea Breeze Clam Fritters

Fried Oysters

Scalloped Oysters

Oven-Fried Fish

Shrimp and Noodles

Salmon Quiche

Salmon Loaf with
  Cream Pea Sauce

Oyster Bake

Tuna and Green Pea Casserole

Salmon-Stuffed Jumbo Shells

Salt Mullets

Milk Gravy

Sauce for Fish

Pork Roast with Yams

3 tablespoons vegetable oil
6–8 pounds pork roast
1 tablespoon dried thyme
2 teaspoons salt
½ cup water

½ teaspoon crushed red pepper
  (optional)
1 can (14 ounces) sauerkraut
4 medium yams, peeled and cut
4 large apples

Preheat oven to 375°. Heat the oil in a roasting pan over medium high heat. Add the roast and turn to brown on all sides, then shake on the thyme and salt and pour in the water. Bake in the oven for 45 minutes. Dip off the fat; you can use a paper towel to help remove it. Put the crushed red pepper, sauerkraut, yams, and apples around the roast. Stir and reduce the heat to 350°. Cover the pan with foil and let cook for 30 minutes more or until done.

Serves 6 to 8.

Stuffed Boneless Pork Loin

Choose a lean pork loin and trim off any excess fat.

5 pounds pork loin

salt

2 teaspoons dried thyme, divided

12 dried plums

1 can (14 ounces) shredded sauerkraut with juice

½ cup water

Preheat oven to 350°. Wash the pork loin under running water. Lay on paper towels on the counter or a cutting board. Split the pork down the center to 1 inch from the bottom; spread the two sides open, leaving them attached. Sprinkle with salt and pat it in. Sprinkle 1 teaspoon of the thyme on the inside. Flatten the dried plums and place them down the center of the loin. Spread the sauerkraut over it. Pull the two sides together and secure them with string or place the loin seam side down in a roasting pan. Sprinkle the remaining thyme over the outside of the loin. Add the water to the pan. Bake, uncovered, for 50 minutes until done.

Serves 6 to 8.

Pork Casserole

2 tablespoons vegetable oil
1 ½ pounds pork tenderloin, cut into strips
1 large sweet onion, sliced and quartered
2 cans (14 ounces each) whole peeled tomatoes
½ teaspoon thyme
½ teaspoon pepper
½ teaspoon salt
1 teaspoon seasoning salt

Heat the oil in a skillet and brown the pork; remove and set aside. Add the onion, tomatoes, and seasonings to the skillet and bring to a boil. Add the pork back in and simmer for 15 to 20 minutes. Serve over rice.

Serves 6.

Oven-Barbecued Baby Back Ribs

5 pounds baby back ribs, cut into
   serving-sized pieces
salt
2 cups vinegar
2 tablespoons Worcestershire sauce
¼ cup brown sugar
½ cup ketchup
½ cup mustard
2 tablespoons seasoning salt
1 teaspoon crushed red pepper
dash of hot pepper sauce

Put the ribs and a pinch of salt in a large pot and cover with water. Bring to a boil and then simmer for 45 minutes. Drain the ribs and set aside. Combine the remaining ingredients to make the sauce and simmer for 15 minutes. Preheat oven to 400°. Lay the ribs in a baking pan and brush them with the sauce. Bake for about 30 minutes, basting frequently.

Serves 6.

Souse Meat

At hog-killing time, the pig's four feet and two ears were boiled and made into a snack. They would be sliced and served with crackers. We would eat them while playing checkers or dominoes. This is an old recipe that is gone but not forgotten!

4 large pig's feet
2–3 pig's ears
2 tablespoons salt
½ teaspoon black pepper
1 teaspoon crushed red pepper

1 tablespoon pickling spice
2 cups apple cider vinegar
¾ cup sweet pickle cubes
¼ cup sugar

Put the feet and ears in a pot and add water to cover by 2 inches. Add the salt, pepper, red pepper, and pickling spice and bring to a boil. Boil for 10 minutes and then turn the heat to low and let simmer until tender, usually about 3½ hours. The meat should fall off the feet bones when done. Remove the meat to cool, reserving 2 cups of the stock. Strain the stock, then add it and the vinegar, pickle cubes, and sugar to a pot and heat. Add the chopped meat and then pour into an 8 × 8-inch pan. Pour stock over the meat and refrigerate until set, about 8 hours.

Serves 8.

Sausage and Green Pepper
Skillet Supper

1½ pounds Italian sausage
3 tablespoons oil
2 medium onions, sliced
2 large green peppers, sliced

1 large red pepper, sliced
1 jar (4½ ounces) sliced
  mushrooms (optional)

Cut sausage on the diagonal into 1-inch pieces. Heat the oil in a skillet over medium heat. Brown the sausage and then remove from pan. Add the onions to the skillet and cook 2 minutes. Add the peppers and stir until hot. Add the mushrooms and return the sausage to the skillet. Stir to mix. Cover and let simmer for 12 minutes. Serve over noodles.

Serves 6.

Baked Beans, Franks, and
Cheese Casserole

1 can (28 ounces) baked beans
¼ cup chopped onion
¼ cup ketchup

3 tablespoons brown sugar
1 pound long franks
1 package (8 ounces) grated cheese

Preheat oven to 375°. Mix the beans, onion, ketchup, and brown sugar in a baking dish. Split the franks lengthwise and press cheese into the middles. Place the franks over the beans and bake 375° for 40 minutes.

Serves 6 to 8.

Cornmeal Gravy

This goes well with salmon patties.

2¾ cups hot milk
3 tablespoons bacon drippings
2 tablespoons cornmeal

1 tablespoon flour
1 teaspoon black pepper
1 teaspoon salt

Heat the milk in a pot. In a frying pan set over medium heat, warm the bacon drippings until hot. Stir in the cornmeal and flour until brown. Add the salt and pepper and then stir in the milk. Turn the heat to low and let simmer, covered, for 20 to 25 minutes.

Makes about 3 cups.

Beef Roasted in a Bag

1 bottom round roast
  (2½–3 pounds)
2 teaspoons seasoning salt
2 medium onions, sliced
3 large carrots, peeled and
  quartered

3 potatoes, peeled and quartered
1 stalk celery, cut into pieces
1 green pepper, sliced and cut
2 cups tomato juice
1 teaspoon garlic salt (optional)

Place the roast in a baking pan. Rub the seasoning salt over it and cover. Let sit at room temperature for 1 hour. Preheat oven to 350°. Place the roast and vegetables in the cooking bag. Pour in the tomato juice and garlic salt and seal the bag. Cook until tender, approximately 1 hour and 15 minutes. Let the roast cool in the bag for 10 to 15 minutes.

Serves 4 to 6.

Chuck Roast

4 pounds chuck roast
1 tablespoon garlic salt
4 tablespoons flour
¼ cup vegetable oil
2 cups water

3 cups diced potato
2 cups diced carrot
2 onions, cut into quarters
2 cups sliced celery

Rub the roast all over with the garlic salt and flour; let set overnight in the refrigerator. Heat the oil in a large roasting pan or stock pot over medium high heat. Add the chuck roast and brown on all sides. Add the water and stir. Cover and let cook for 1 hour. Add the potato, carrot, onion, and celery. Cover and let cook for 1 hour. Check for seasoning.

Serves 6.

Old-Fashioned Corned Beef Hash

This can be served for breakfast or brunch. The country name for this dish was "Slain Hatchet."

½ stick butter or margarine
1½ pounds ground chuck or lean ground beef
1 cup chopped onion
1 can (15¼ ounces) yellow corn, drained
2 cups diced potato, cooked and drained
1 teaspoon seasoning salt

Preheat oven to 375°. Melt the butter in a skillet and brown the meat and onion. Stir in the corn and potato and cook until hot. Add the salt. Put in a baking dish and bake for 15 minutes.

Serves 6 to 8.

Country-Style Hamburger Steak

This can be served with rice and green peas and fruit Jell-O.

1½ pounds ground sirloin
2 teaspoons vegetable oil
2 eggs, beaten
¼ cup bread crumbs
1 teaspoon garlic salt
½ stick butter or margarine

3 medium onions, sliced
2 cups sliced mushrooms
2 tablespoons flour
1 can (14½ ounces) beef broth
2 cups water

In a bowl, combine the first five ingredients until well blended. Shape the mixture into 4 oblong patties. Melt the butter in a skillet over medium heat and add the patties. Brown on both sides and remove from the pan. Add the onions and mushrooms to the pan and cook 8 to 10 minutes. Do not brown. Stir in the flour and let brown, then pour in the broth and water to make a gravy. Let this cook to thicken, approximately 12 to 15 minutes, then add the cooked patties and simmer for 8 minutes. Serve the gravy over the patties.

Serves 4.

Meat Loaf

2 pounds ground beef
2 cups bread crumbs, grated
  or chopped fine
1 package onion soup mix

½ cup finely chopped green pepper
2 eggs, beaten
¼ cup milk

Preheat oven to 350°. Blend all of the ingredients together. Press the mixture into a greased loaf pan and bake 50 minutes or until done. When done, turn off the oven and let the meatloaf sit inside it for 15 minutes.

Serves 6 to 8.

Meat Loaf with Horseradish and Mushrooms

¾ cup crushed saltine crackers
3 eggs, beaten
½ cup ketchup
2 tablespoons horseradish
1 teaspoon seasoning salt
¾ stick butter

½ cup chopped onion
2 pounds lean ground beef
1 jar (12 ounces) mushrooms,
  drained and chopped
¾ cup sour cream

Preheat oven to 375°. In a bowl, combine the crackers, eggs, ketchup, horseradish, and salt. Heat the butter in a saucepan on medium heat. Add the onions and cook, stirring, about 3 minutes; do not brown. Mix the onion and ground beef into the cracker mixture. Stir in the mushrooms and sour cream until well blended. Press the mixture into a 9 × 5-inch loaf pan. Bake for 1 hour until done.

Serves 6 to 8.

Meat Loaf in a Blanket

Serve with brown beef gravy (see the following recipe).

2 pounds lean ground beef
1 large egg, beaten
¼ cup finely chopped onion
¼ cup brown beef gravy
   (see recipe below)
1 teaspoon garlic salt

1 cup bread crumbs
½ cup milk
1 can refrigerated biscuits
melted butter or margarine for
   brushing biscuits

Preheat oven to 375°. In a bowl, mix together the beef, egg, onion, gravy, garlic salt, bread crumbs, and milk. Press the mixture into a loaf pan and bake for 45 minutes, until done. Take the meatloaf from the oven and dip out the fat. Roll or press out the biscuits and spread them evenly over the top and sides of the meat loaf. Prick the sides with a fork and bake until brown; remove and brush with butter or margarine. Serve with brown beef gravy.

Serves 6 to 8.

Brown Beef Gravy

3 tablespoons vegetable oil or
   bacon drippings
3 tablespoons flour
1 can (14½ ounces) beef broth
½ cup water

1 can (4½ ounces) sliced
   mushrooms, drained (optional)
1 can (8½ ounces) green peas,
   drained (optional)
salt and black pepper to taste

Heat the oil in a frying pan. Add the flour and stir until brown; lower the heat. Stir in the broth and water, then simmer 10 to 12 minutes, adding a little more water if needed. Add the mushrooms and peas, if desired. Add salt and pepper to taste.

Makes about 3 cups.

Hamburger Goulash

2 pounds ground beef
2 garlic cloves, chopped fine
1 cup chopped green pepper
½ cup finely chopped onion
2 cans (14½ ounces each) diced
   tomatoes, with juices

1 pound rigatoni, prepared as
   directed
Parmesan cheese

Cook the ground beef in a large skillet over medium high heat, stirring until done. Remove the meat to a colander to drain, leaving a little fat in the skillet. Add the garlic, pepper, and onion to the skillet and cook for 2 to 3 minutes. Stir in the tomatoes, beef, and rigatoni. Reduce the heat to low and cover. Cook until heated through, adding a little water if needed. Sprinkle with freshly ground Parmesan cheese.

Serves 6.

Shepherd's Pie

2 tablespoons vegetable oil
½ cup chopped onion
½ cup finely chopped carrot
1½ pounds ground beef
1 can (10½ ounces) cream of
  mushroom soup

2 tablespoons flour
¼ cup tomato sauce
1 can refrigerated biscuits
  (or mashed potatoes) for
  topping

Preheat oven to 400°. Heat the oil in a skillet over medium heat and add the onions, cooking 3 to 4 minutes. Add the carrot and ground beef and cook until done, 12 to 15 minutes. Add the soup. Stir in the flour and tomato sauce. Bring to a simmer and cook for 5 minutes. Pour into a baking dish and top with the biscuits.

Potatoes can be used as an alternative to biscuits for the topping. Peel 1½ pounds of potatoes and boil until tender. Mash the potatoes with ½ stick of butter and 1 teaspoon garlic salt. Spread over the beef mixture and top with shredded cheddar cheese. Bake for 20 minutes.

Serves 6.

Beef-o-Roni

This dish is also good left over for the next day!

2 tablespoons vegetable oil
½ cup chopped onion
1 cup chopped green pepper
1½ pounds ground beef
2 cans (14½ ounces each)
  stewed tomatoes

1 teaspoon seasoning salt
¼ cup grated Parmesan cheese
1 pound rigatoni or elbow
  macaroni

Heat the oil in a large pot. Add the onion and pepper and cook 3 to 4 minutes. Do not brown. Add the beef, stirring until the meat crumbles, and cook until done. Drain off the excess fat and put in the tomatoes, seasoning salt, cheese, and rigatoni. Cover and cook slowly for 20 to 25 minutes until the noodles are tender.

Serves 6.

Porcupine Meatballs

1½ pounds ground beef
¾ cup cooked rice
1 teaspoon garlic salt
dash hot sauce
2 tablespoons chopped
   sweet onion

1 can (10½ ounces) cream of
   tomato soup
1 can (10½ ounces) cream of
   mushroom soup
1 cup water

Preheat oven to 375°. Mix together the ground beef, rice, garlic salt, hot sauce, and onion. Shape the mixture into balls and place them in a baking dish. Cover and bake for 20 minutes. Remove from the oven and pour off the fat from the baking dish. Pour the soups and water over the meatballs. Return the dish to the oven and bake until bubbling hot, 12 to 15 minutes.

Serves 6.

Hamburger, Macaroni, and Cheese Casserole

¼ cup vegetable oil
1 pound ground beef
½ cup chopped onion
¼ cup water
1 tablespoon Worcestershire sauce
1 can (14½ ounces) diced tomatoes

1 teaspoon seasoning salt
1 teaspoon sugar
1 box (16 ounces) macaroni,
    prepared as directed
1 cup cracker crumbs
4 tablespoons butter, melted

Preheat oven to 375°. Heat the oil in a skillet and brown the ground beef with the onion. Drain off the excess fat and stir in the water, Worcestershire sauce, tomatoes, salt, sugar, and macaroni. Mix well and pour into a 1½-quart baking dish. Combine the cracker crumbs and butter and sprinkle over the casserole. Bake for 20 minutes.

Serves 6.

Spaghetti Sauce

1 ½ pounds ground beef
1 cup finely chopped onion
½ cup finely chopped green pepper
½ cup chopped celery
3 garlic cloves, finely chopped
2 cans (14½ ounces each) diced
   tomatoes, finely chopped,
   with juice

2 cans (8 ounces each) tomato sauce
1 tablespoon sugar
1 tablespoon Italian seasoning
2 tablespoons chili powder
1 can (4 ounces) sliced black olives
¼ cup grated Parmesan cheese

Brown the ground beef over medium high heat until crumbly. Drain off the fat. Add the onion, green pepper, celery, and garlic and stir until softened. Reduce the heat if necessary. Add the remaining ingredients and bring to a boil. Reduce the heat to low and simmer for 15 to 20 minutes. Serve over spaghetti noodles.

Serves 4 to 6.

Lasagna

2 tablespoons vegetable oil
2 teaspoons minced garlic
¼ cup chopped onion
2 pounds ground beef
2 teaspoons seasoning salt
2 cans (8 ounces each) tomato
   sauce
2 cans (14½ ounces each) diced
   tomatoes
1 container (16 ounces) ricotta
   cheese

1 small container (8 ounces)
   cottage cheese
1 small can (5 ounces)
   evaporated milk
1 box (16 ounces) lasagna,
   prepared as directed
½ pound mozzarella cheese,
   grated
½ cup grated Parmesan cheese

Preheat oven to 375°. Add the oil, garlic, and onion to a large pot
and cook for 2 minutes. Do not brown. Add the ground beef and salt,
cooking until the beef is done. Pour off some of the fat. Add the tomato
sauce and tomatoes, stirring until combined, and let cook 20 minutes.
Mix together the ricotta cheese, cottage cheese, and evaporated milk.
In a 9 × 13 × 3-inch baking dish alternate the cooked noodles with the
mozzarella cheese and the sauce to make three complete layers, ending
with the sauce. Sprinkle the Parmesan cheese on top. Cover and bake
for 40 minutes, then uncover and bake until brown.

Serves 8 to 10.

Spinach Lasagna

This is a good vegetarian dish.

2 large eggs

1 large container (16 ounces) cottage cheese

2 teaspoons garlic salt

2 boxes (10 ounces each) frozen chopped spinach, cooked as directed

½ stick butter, melted

2 packages (8 ounces each) shredded Monterey Jack and Colby cheese

1 cup grated Parmesan cheese, divided

1 box (16 ounces) lasagna, cooked as directed

Preheat oven to 350°. Mix together the eggs, cottage cheese, and garlic salt in a bowl. Combine the spinach, butter, shredded cheese, and half of the Parmesan cheese. Spread a small amount of the egg mixture in a 9 × 13 × 2-inch baking dish and then add alternating layers of the noodles, egg mixture, and spinach mixture, ending with the spinach mixture. Sprinkle the remaining Parmesan cheese on top and bake for 30 to 40 minutes.

Serves 8 to 10.

Breaded Veal Cutlets

4 veal cutlets
1 cup all-purpose flour
1 cup dry bread crumbs
¼ teaspoon salt
¼ teaspoon black pepper

1 cup milk
2 eggs, beaten
½ cup vegetable oil
½ cup water

Pound the cutlets until thin. Mix together the flour, bread crumbs, salt, and pepper. Mix the milk and eggs; beat to combine. Heat the oil in a large skillet over medium high heat. Coat the veal in the milk mixture and then the flour mixture. Add the veal to the skillet and cook until brown on both sides. Add the water; reduce the heat and simmer for about 20 minutes until tender. Taste for seasoning.

Serves 4.

Roasted Chicken

1 roasting chicken (4–5 pounds)
1 tablespoon plus 2 teaspoons salt
½ teaspoon dried thyme
¾ stick butter or margarine, softened
1 stalk celery, cut into pieces
1 onion, quartered

Place the chicken in a large pan or in the sink and sprinkle it with one tablespoon of the salt. Let it sit for 25 minutes, then rinse and pat dry with paper towels.

Preheat oven to 350°. Sprinkle the inside cavity of the chicken with the thyme and salt. Add half the butter, the celery, and the onion. Rub the outside of the chicken with the remaining butter. Tuck the wing tips under the back of the chicken and place it breast side down on a rack in a roasting pan. Roast for 20 minutes; turn the chicken breast side up and roast for another 45 minutes or until tender.

Serves 6 to 8.

Roast Capon with Dressing

My favorite chicken in the South is the capon, which is often in stores around the holidays. You will find them in the frozen section with hens, ducks, and turkeys. Serve the roast capon with gravy made from the pan drippings (see the following recipe).

1 capon (7–8 pounds)	butter
3 tablespoons salt	vegetable oil

Dressing

½ cup chopped onions	1 can (10½ ounces) chicken broth
½ cup chopped celery	1 cup water
1 stick butter, melted	½ teaspoon sage
3 cups dry bread crumbs	½ teaspoon poultry seasoning
1 cup cracker crumbs	

Thaw the capon in the refrigerator about 2 days. Fill the sink with cold water and mix in the salt. Add the capon, breast side up. Remove the neck and giblets, reserving the giblets for the gravy. After an hour of soaking, turn the capon breast side down. Wash the cavity and neck area. Drain the water from the capon and pat it dry with paper towels.

Preheat oven to 325°. Combine all of the dressing ingredients and mix well. Fill the cavity loosely with dressing and place the stuffed capon breast side up on a rack in a roasting pan. Rub the skin heavily with melted butter mixed with oil. Bake, uncovered, 35 minutes per pound, basting frequently with the pan juices.

Capon Gravy

capon giblets
pan drippings from roast capon
3 tablespoons flour
4 cups water

Simmer the giblets in water until tender; drain and chop. Pour 3 to 4 tablespoons of fat from the roasting pan into a saucepan set over medium heat. Add the flour and stir until brown. Pour the water into the roasting pan and stir, then pour the liquid into the saucepan. Mix well and raise the heat to simmer 12 to 15 minutes. Add the chopped gizzards and liver.

Serves 6 to 8.

Baked Hen

Hens were served at the country table in many dishes before turkey became popular. We stewed them or made chicken pastry, chicken and dumplings, or chicken salad. The roosters we left to crow in the morning. My Aunt Laura would always remind me to make sure I got the hen securely under my arms to carry it home.

The hen must first be singed to remove the hairy feathers. At the sink, hold the hen over a flame, turning to singe it all over. Pat the hen with 1 tablespoon salt. Let sit for 20 to 30 minutes, then rinse under running water. Preheat oven to 350°. Rub salt and butter over the hen's skin and place it in a baking pan with 3 stalks of celery cut into pieces. Cook for 2 ½ to 3 hours, basting after each hour. Check the thighs for tenderness.

Serves 6 to 8.

Braised Chicken

1 roasting chicken (4−5 pounds)
1 tablespoon seasoning salt
1 teaspoon black pepper
½ stick butter
1 cup sliced carrots

1 cup sliced onions
1 cup sliced celery
1 can (14½ ounces) chicken broth
½ tablespoon poultry seasoning

Preheat oven to 350°. Wash the chicken, pat it dry, and place it in a roasting pan. Sprinkle the inside and outside of the chicken with the seasoning salt and pepper then rub it inside and out with the butter. Add the vegetables, broth, and poultry seasoning to the pan and cover. Cook for 1 hour until the chicken is fork tender and the juices run clear. Remove the chicken to a platter and surround with the vegetables.

Serves 6.

Chicken Tetrazzini

1 hen or roasting chicken
  (6 pounds)
1 teaspoon seasoning salt
1 bay leaf
½ pound spaghetti
1 can (10 ounces) chicken broth
½ stick butter

½ cup chopped onion
1 cup diced green pepper
1 cup diced celery
2 cans (10½ ounces each) cream
  of mushroom soup
¼ cup freshly grated Parmesan
  cheese

Wash the chicken and remove the giblets, freezing for later use. Put the chicken in a large pot and add water to cover by 2 inches. Add the seasoning salt and bay leaf. Cook over medium heat until done, approximately 45 minutes. Remove the chicken from the pot, reserving the stock. When the chicken is cool, remove the skin and bones. Chop the chicken and set aside. Skim the fat from the stock; strain and set aside. Cook the spaghetti in the chicken broth until tender. Heat the butter in a saucepan and cook the onion, green pepper, and celery until tender. Put half of the spaghetti in a 2½-quart baking dish. Spread half the chicken and vegetables evenly over the spaghetti. Repeat with the remaining spaghetti, chicken, and vegetables. Pour the cream of mushroom soup and the reserved stock over the dish. Cover with the Parmesan cheese. Bake at 350° for 35 minutes.

Serves 6 to 8.

Chicken Tortilla Stew

If you are having trouble making homemade chicken and dumplings, this is a good substitute.

1 broiler chicken (3½–4 pounds)
2 cans (14½ ounces each) chicken broth
¾ stick butter
1 tablespoon dried parsley (optional)
7 10-inch flour tortillas

Wash the chicken in salt water, put it breast side down in a large pot, and cover it with water. Bring the water to a boil and reduce the heat to medium. Let cook (but not boil) until the chicken is tender, turning the chicken over after about 40 minutes to cook evenly. Let the chicken begin to cool down in the pot, then remove to a bowl to finish cooling. When cool, pull the meat from the bone. Cut or pull the meat into strips. Skim the fat from the stock and strain. Add enough canned broth to the stock to make six cups total; pour the liquid into a pot. Add the butter and parsley. Cut the tortillas in 1½-inch squares. When the pot begins to boil, alternately add the chicken and tortillas, stirring after each addition. Simmer for 10 minutes.

Serves 6 to 8.

Honey Mustard Chicken Breast

⅓ cup mustard
⅓ cup honey
¼ stick butter or margarine
1 teaspoon dried dill, chopped

1 cup frozen orange juice
concentrate
4 chicken breasts

Preheat oven to 400°. Combine the mustard, honey, butter, dill, and orange juice concentrate in a bowl. Place the chicken breast side up on a baking pan. Brush the top of the chicken with the sauce, coating well. Turn the chicken over and brush with the remaining sauce. Bake until done, about 30 minutes.

Serves 4 to 6.

Marinated Drumsticks

10 drumsticks
1 tablespoon salt
1 teaspoon garlic salt
4 teaspoons soy sauce

2 tablespoons plus 2 cups
vegetable oil
¾ cup self-rising flour

Wash the drumsticks in 1 quart cold water with the salt. Rinse off and pat dry. Mix the garlic salt, soy sauce, and 2 tablespoons oil in one bowl; put the flour in another bowl. Dip the drumsticks into the seasoning mixture and then into the flour to coat, shaking off any excess. Refrigerate the drumsticks for two hours or overnight. Add the 2 cups oil to a pan on medium high. Working in 2 batches, fry the drumsticks until brown.

Serves 4 to 5.

Fruity Chicken

6 chicken thighs or drumsticks
1 cup flour
½ teaspoon salt
½ teaspoon black pepper
vegetable oil for frying
1 cup orange juice
1 can sliced apricots

1 cup dried plums
2 tablespoons brown sugar
3 tablespoons apple cider vinegar
1 teaspoon allspice
1 teaspoon dried basil
1 teaspoon garlic salt

Wash the chicken in salt water; rinse and pat dry. Mix the flour with the salt and pepper and set aside. Heat the oil in a skillet over medium high heat. Batter the chicken in the flour mixture and fry until brown on both sides. Remove the chicken from the pan and pour off all the oil but 2 tablespoons. Put the chicken back in the skillet and pour the juice, apricots, and plums over it. Add the sugar, vinegar, and remaining seasonings and let simmer 20 to 25 minutes.

Serves 6.

Spicy Hot Chicken Thighs

6 chicken thighs
½ cup vegetable oil
1 cup apple cider vinegar
1 cup brown sugar
3 tablespoons hot sauce

1 tablespoon garlic salt
½ teaspoon cayenne pepper
1 can (14½ ounces)
    stewed tomatoes

Preheat oven to 325°. Wash the chicken in salt water and pat dry. Heat the oil in a skillet over medium high heat and brown both sides of the thighs. Put the chicken in a roasting pan and bake for 30 minutes. Remove the pan from the oven and drain off the liquid. In a bowl, combine all the other ingredients and pour over the chicken. Return the pan to the oven, raise the temperature to 400°, and bake for 35 more minutes.

Serves 6.

Creole Chicken Thighs

6–8 chicken thighs
½ cup vegetable oil or margarine
¾ cup sliced and quartered onions
1 tablespoon flour
1 can (15 ounces) crushed tomatoes
1 can (8 ounces) tomato sauce

1 cup shredded Parmesan cheese
2 teaspoons garlic salt
2 teaspoons Cajun seasoning
½ teaspoon dried thyme
1 teaspoon hot sauce
salt to taste

Wash the chicken in salt water and pat dry. Heat the oil in a skillet over medium high heat and add the chicken, browning on both sides. Remove the thighs from the pan and pour off all but 3 tablespoons of the oil. Add the onion to the pan and cook, stirring, about 4 minutes. Stir in the flour. Mix in the tomatoes, tomato sauce, and cheese. Add the spices; reduce the heat and simmer for 20 to 30 minutes. Serve over rice.

Serves 6.

Country-Style Smothered Chicken Gizzards

2 pounds chicken gizzards
½ cup vegetable oil
1 cup + 1 tablespoon flour

1 teaspoon black pepper
1 can (10½ ounces) chicken broth
1 cup water

Wash the gizzards in salt water. Heat the oil in a skillet over medium high heat. In a bowl, mix together 1 cup of the flour and the pepper. Batter the gizzards in the flour mixture and fry until brown on all sides. Remove the gizzards from the pan and pour off all the oil but 2 tablespoons. Add the tablespoon of flour and stir until brown. Stir in the chicken broth and water and cook until hot. Add the gizzards and simmer for 30 minutes until tender. Serve over rice.

Serves 5 to 6.

Turkey à la King

You can also buy turkey or chicken parts to make this dish instead of using the meat left over from a whole roasted turkey.

¼ stick butter or margarine
¼ cup flour
4 cups turkey stock (see below)
1 large can (12 ounces)
   evaporated milk
1 jar (8 ounces) sliced mushrooms,
   drained, with juice reserved

3 tablespoons pimento
4 cups diced turkey
salt and black pepper to taste
3 hard-boiled eggs, sliced
   or chopped

Heat the butter in a large pot for 2 to 3 minutes. Add the flour and stir to mix; do not brown. Pour in the stock, evaporated milk, and mushroom juice and bring to a boil. Cook for 2 minutes and add the mushrooms, pimento, and turkey, cooking until very hot. Put in the eggs, stir, and simmer for about 3 minutes. Serve on rice or toast.

To make the stock, remove the leftover meat from a whole roasted turkey; dice and set aside. Put the bones in a large pot with 2 4-inch pieces of celery, half of a small onion, and 1 bay leaf. Cover with 6 cups of water. Bring to a boil, turn the heat to low, and cook slowly for 1 hour or more. Remove the bones, strain the stock, and add enough water to make 4 cups.

Serves 6 to 8.

Chicken Noodle Pie

2 cups chicken broth
1 can (10½ ounces) cream of
  chicken soup
1 stick butter
3 pounds chopped, cooked chicken
1 package (16 ounces) egg noodles,
  cooked as directed

1 can large refrigerated buttermilk
  biscuits
milk or melted butter for brushing
  tops of biscuits

Preheat oven to 425°. Heat the broth, soup, and butter together in a pot until the butter melts. Combine the chicken, noodles, and broth mixture and pour into a 13 × 9 × 2-inch baking pan. Place the biscuits over the chicken mixture and brush with milk or butter. Bake until golden brown, approximately 25 minutes.

Serves 6.

Chicken Croquettes

1 cup milk
2 tablespoons flour
2 tablespoons water
2 tablespoons butter or margarine
½ teaspoon seasoning salt
2 cups cooked chicken,
  finely chopped

1 tablespoon sweet onion
1 cup bread crumbs
1 egg, beaten
1 cup flour or Shake and Bake
  for coating

Preheat oven to 375°. Heat the milk in a saucepan. Mix the flour with the water to form a paste and stir into the milk, cooking until thickened. Add the butter. Let cool. Add the seasoning salt. Add the chicken, onion, bread crumbs, and egg. Form the mixture into croquettes. Coat the croquettes with flour and bake until brown, approximately 30 minutes.

Serves 5.

Chicken Noodle Casserole

1½ pounds chicken breast

1 package (16 ounces) egg noodles, cooked as directed

2 cans (10½ ounces each) cream of chicken soup

1 container (8 ounces) sour cream

1 can (8 ounces) sliced mushrooms

2 cups cracker crumbs

½ stick butter or margarine, melted

Preheat oven to 350°. Wash the chicken and put it in a pot with water to cover. Cook over medium heat until tender, about 45 minutes. Remove the chicken to cool, then pull the meat from the bone and cut into pieces. Strain the broth (there should be about 2 cups) and set aside. In a bowl, combine the noodles with the broth, cream of chicken soup, sour cream, mushrooms, and chicken. Pour the mixture into a baking dish. Mix the cracker crumbs with the butter and sprinkle over the casserole. Bake for 30 minutes until bubbling hot and crispy brown. Serve with salad or fruit.

Serves 6 to 8.

Chicken Noodle Casserole with Tortilla Crust

1 can (14½ ounces) chicken broth
1½ pounds chicken breast
½ package (8 ounces) egg noodles, cooked as directed
1 can (10½ ounces) cream of chicken soup

1 stick butter, melted
2 flour tortillas, cut into 1-inch strips

Preheat oven to 425°. Heat the broth in a saucepan and cook the chicken until tender. Strain the broth and set it aside. Cut the chicken into pieces and place on the bottom of a 9 × 13-inch baking pan. Add the noodles to the pan. Mix together the soup, butter, and broth and pour over the noodles. Butter the tortillas and spread over the noodles as a topping. Bake until topping is brown and crunchy, about 30 minutes.

Serves 6.

Turkey Noodle Casserole

2 tablespoons vegetable oil
½ cup chopped onion
¼ cup chopped celery
1½ pounds ground turkey
2 tablespoons flour
1 can (14½ ounces) chicken broth

1 cup sour cream
4 ounces grated cheddar cheese
1 package (16 ounces) egg noodles,
    cooked as directed
2 cups cracker crumbs
2 tablespoons butter, melted

Preheat oven to 375°. Add the oil, onion, and celery to a skillet set over medium heat. Cook, stirring, for 4 to 5 minutes. Stir in the turkey, cooking until done. Stir in the flour and add the chicken broth, sour cream, and cheese. Mix in the noodles. Pour into a baking dish and sprinkle with the cracker crumbs and butter. Bake for 25 minutes.

Serves 6.

Barbecue Turkey Franks

This dish is good with baked beans and coleslaw or corn.

1 package turkey franks
3 tablespoons vegetable oil
¼ cup chopped onion
2 tablespoons brown sugar
1 teaspoon mustard

½ cup ketchup
¼ cup cider vinegar
1 tablespoon Worcestershire sauce
2 tablespoons chili powder

Preheat oven to 375°. Cut the franks into 1-inch pieces and put in a baking dish. Heat the oil in a saucepan and sauté the onions over medium heat until tender but not brown. Put in all other ingredients and let simmer for 15 to 20 minutes. Pour the mixture over the franks. Bake for 30 minutes.

Serves 6 to 8.

Giblet Gravy

1 package chicken giblets
   (heart, gizzard, liver)
¼ cup vegetable oil

3 tablespoons flour
2½ cups chicken broth
salt and black pepper to taste

Boil the giblets in water until tender; drain and chop. Heat the oil in a saucepan on medium high, add the flour, and stir until brown. Stir in the chicken broth and add the giblets. Cover the pan, reduce the heat to low, and let simmer for 25 minutes. Add a little hot water if needed. Add salt and pepper to taste.

Makes about 2½ cups.

Crab Cakes I

3 slices day-old bread,
   crusts removed
¼ cup milk
2 eggs, beaten
2 tablespoons mayonnaise
½ teaspoon salt

1 tablespoon mustard
½ pound fresh crabmeat,
   picked over
⅓ cup saltine cracker crumbs
½ cup vegetable oil

Lay the bread slices on a baking sheet and put in a warm oven about
2 hours. (For gas ovens, the heat from the pilot light is sufficient.)
Remove and grate into a bowl. Add the milk, eggs, mayonnaise, salt,
and mustard and mix well. Add the crabmeat and stir lightly until just
blended. Refrigerate for 1 hour or more. Remove and shape the mixture
into patties. Roll each patty in the cracker crumbs. Heat the oil in a
pan over medium high and brown the patties on both sides. Remove to
paper towels to drain.

Serves 5.

Crab Cakes II

1 pound fresh crabmeat,
  picked over
1 egg, beaten
1 teaspoon Worcestershire sauce
2 tablespoons mayonnaise
1 tablespoon mustard

1 tablespoon butter, melted
1 teaspoon garlic salt
½ cup bread crumbs
1 cup saltine cracker crumbs
vegetable oil for frying

Combine all the ingredients in a bowl and mix well. Sprinkle half the cracker crumbs on a sheet of aluminum foil. Form the crab mixture into patties and lightly batter them in the cracker crumbs, turning with a spatula to coat both sides. Heat the oil on medium high, then lift the crab cakes with a spatula and slide them into the pan. Brown on both sides; remove to paper towels to drain.

Serves 4 to 6.

Country Fish Cakes

This can be a breakfast or a supper dish.

2 pounds catfish or sea bass fillets
2 teaspoons salt, divided
1 teaspoon vegetable oil + oil
   for frying
2 large eggs, beaten
¼ cup mayonnaise
3 tablespoons milk

2 sleeves saltine crackers, crushed
3 cups self-rising flour
1 teaspoon black pepper
1 tablespoon mustard
1 tablespoon Worcestershire sauce
1 teaspoon seafood seasoning

Preheat oven to 350°. Sprinkle the fillets with 1 teaspoon of the salt and brush with the oil. Lay the fish on a baking pan and bake for 18 minutes. Cool the fillets and crumble them into small pieces in a bowl. Add the eggs, mayonnaise, milk, and cracker crumbs, and mix well. Shape the mixture into patties and place them on a sheet pan; refrigerate for about an hour. Mix together the flour, remaining salt, pepper, mustard, Worcestershire sauce, and seafood seasoning. Spread the flour mixture over a piece of foil with a spatula. Lay the fish cakes on the foil, turning them with a spatula and sprinkling the flour mixture around the edges. Handling the cakes lightly and without crowding the pan, fry them in hot oil until brown on both sides. Drain on paper towels.

Serves 6 to 8.

Sea Breeze Clam Fritters

4 cans (6½ ounces each) minced
    clams, drained
1 tablespoon chopped onion
2 eggs, beaten

2 tablespoons self-rising flour
½ teaspoon seasoning salt
black pepper to taste
1 cup vegetable oil

Combine the clams and onion. Add the eggs, flour, salt, and pepper and
mix together until well blended. Form the mixture into small cakes
and fry in hot oil until brown on both sides. Drain on paper towels.

Serves 4 to 5.

Fried Oysters

Keep the oysters very cold until ready to cook them.

2 eggs, beaten
¾ cup milk
12 oysters
2 cups saltine cracker crumbs

½ cup self-rising flour
1 teaspoon salt
vegetable oil for frying

Combine the eggs and milk in a bowl and mix well. Add the oysters
and stir to coat. On a baking pan, mix together the cracker crumbs,
flour, and salt. Batter one oyster at a time. Heat the oil in a frying
pan on medium heat. To test oil temperature, drop in a few cracker
crumbs; if they sizzle the oil is hot enough. Add the oysters, without
overcrowding the pan, and fry to your liking—crispy or soft.

Serves 4.

Scalloped Oysters

This is a good side dish with turkey at Thanksgiving or any time.

3 cups saltine cracker crumbs

1 large can (12 ounces) evaporated milk, plus enough water to make 2 cups

1 stick butter, melted

1 quart oysters, cut in half

¼ teaspoon salt

black pepper to taste

Preheat oven to 400°. Butter a 1½-quart baking dish and spread half the cracker crumbs over the bottom. Spoon in half the evaporated milk and then half the butter. Add the oysters and sprinkle with salt and pepper. Add the rest of the cracker crumbs. Spoon the remaining butter and evaporated milk over the top. Bake for 25 to 30 minutes.

Serves 6.

Oven-Fried Fish

¼ cup milk

1 egg, beaten

1½ pounds perch fillets

¼ cup self-rising cornmeal

¼ teaspoon salt

¼ teaspoon cayenne pepper

black pepper (optional)

vegetable oil

Preheat oven to 400°. Mix the milk and egg together well. Cover the fish with the milk mixture and set aside for 10 minutes. Mix the cornmeal with the salt, cayenne pepper, and black pepper. Remove the fish from the milk mixture, coat with the cornmeal, and place on an oiled baking pan. Drizzle on a little oil and bake uncovered for 20 to 30 minutes until the fish is flaky.

Serves 4.

Shrimp and Noodles

1 tablespoon vegetable oil
3 pounds medium shrimp,
  peeled and deveined
1 package (16 ounces) spinach
  noodles, cook as directed

1 cup sour cream
1 cup mayonnaise
freshly grated sharp cheese

Preheat oven to 300°. Heat the oil in a frying pan over medium high. Add the shrimp and sauté until pink. Put the noodles in a large baking pan, and spoon the shrimp (without the liquids) over the top. Combine the sour cream and mayonnaise and mix well; pour over the noodles. Top with the cheese. Bake for 30 minutes.

Serves 6 to 8.

Salmon Quiche

1 9-inch deep dish pie shell,
  baked at 400° for 8 minutes
2 tablespoons butter, margarine,
  or vegetable oil
3 tablespoons sliced spring onion,
  white part only
4 large eggs

2 tablespoons mayonnaise
½ cup sour cream
½ teaspoon dried dill
1 can (14¾ ounces) pink salmon,
  drained, bones and skin removed
1½ cups grated Swiss cheese

Heat the butter in a pan and sauté the onions about 3 minutes. Do not brown. Beat the eggs in a bowl. Stir in the butter and onions until blended. Add the mayonnaise, sour cream, and dill, and crumble in the salmon. Spread the cheese in the pie shell and then pour the salmon mixture over the cheese. Bake at 400° for 40 minutes until brown. Cool for 10 minutes before cutting.

Serves 6 to 10.

Salmon Loaf with Cream Pea Sauce

1 can (14¾ ounces) pink salmon
¾ cup milk
3 tablespoon chopped spring
  onion, white part only
2 eggs, beaten

1½ cups bread crumbs
½ stick butter or margarine
½ teaspoon seasoning salt
½ teaspoon dried dill

Sauce

3 tablespoons butter
3 tablespoons flour
1 cup of milk
liquid from salmon

1 tablespoon mayonnaise
1 small can (8½ ounces)
  green peas

Preheat oven to 350°. Drain the salmon, reserving the liquid for the sauce. Remove the skin and bones. Put the salmon in a bowl, add all the other ingredients, and mix well. Put the mixture in a greased 5 × 9-inch loaf pan. Mash to pack tight. Bake for 50 minutes.

To make the sauce, melt the butter in a saucepan. Stir in the flour and blend well. Do not brown. Add the milk and the liquid from the salmon. Stir in the mayonnaise. Cook, stirring, until the sauce thickens. Stir in the green peas. Pour over the salmon loaf.

Oyster Bake

I suggest that you serve this warm on toast rounds as an hors d'oeuvre.

4 tablespoons butter, divided
¼ cup sliced spring onions
1 box (10 ounces) frozen creamed
    spinach, cooked and drained
20 large oysters, rinsed

1 dollop hot sauce (optional)
salt and black pepper to taste
1 cup cracker crumbs
¼ cup Parmesan cheese (optional)

Preheat oven to 450°. Butter a 9 × 13-inch baking dish. Melt 2 tablespoons of the butter in a skillet and sauté the onions until softened.
Spread the spinach over the bottom of the pan, place the oysters
on top, and sprinkle them with the onions. Dot with hot sauce and
then sprinkle with salt and pepper to taste. Mix the remaining 2
tablespoons butter with the cracker crumbs and sprinkle on top
with the cheese. Bake for about 10 minutes.

Serves 10, 4 to 5 oysters per serving.

Tuna and Green Pea Casserole

1 package (16 ounces) egg noodles, cooked as directed

3 cans (6 ounces each) tuna, with liquid

1 box (10 ounces) frozen green peas, thawed

2 cups grated cheddar cheese

2 cups milk

2 tablespoons cornstarch

½ teaspoon salt

½ teaspoon black pepper

½ cup cracker crumbs

2 tablespoons butter, melted

Preheat oven to 375°. In a 2-quart baking dish, mix the noodles, tuna, and peas. In a saucepan, heat the cheese and milk until the cheese melts, then stir in the cornstarch. Add to the noodle mixture along with the salt and pepper and stir lightly to mix. Combine the cracker crumbs and butter and sprinkle over the casserole. Bake for 25 minutes on lower rack of oven.

Serves 6.

Salmon-Stuffed Jumbo Shells

These can be served with a good tomato sauce or as an hors d'oeuvre.

1 pound fresh salmon
2 tablespoons vegetable oil
salt and black pepper to taste
1 teaspoon lemon juice
3 tablespoons basil vinegar
2 tablespoons sliced spring onions

1 cup zucchini, sliced and cut
   into thin strips
1 firm tomato, seeded and diced
2 tablespoons cider vinegar
20 jumbo pasta shells,
   cooked as directed

Preheat oven to 400°. Rub the salmon with the oil and place on a
baking pan. Sprinkle with salt, pepper, and lemon juice. Bake for
15 to 20 minutes, then check for doneness. Let cool and remove the
skin. Flake the meat into a bowl. Toss together with all the other
ingredients except the shells and taste for seasonings. Spoon 1
generous tablespoon of the mixture into each shell and serve.

Serves 5 to 6.

Salt Mullets

*We often had salt fish (fish that had been preserved in salt) for breakfast on
Saturday mornings with scrambled eggs and milk gravy. Papa would bring
the fish home on Wednesday. They were cleaned and washed and put in a big
pan of cold water. We changed the water every day until Saturday. The fish
were battered in cornmeal and fried slowly until crisp to the bones.*

Milk Gravy

We always made this gravy with fatback bacon drippings.

3 tablespoons fat drippings
3 tablespoons flour
2 cups hot milk
salt and black pepper to taste

Heat the drippings and stir in the flour. Cook over low heat until browned but not burned. Gradually add the milk, stirring constantly, until the gravy is thickened. Season with salt and pepper to taste. Add a little water or ½ stick of butter or margarine if needed.

Makes about 1 ¼ cups.

Sauce for Fish

½ cup chili sauce
½ cup ketchup
⅓ cup horseradish

¼ teaspoon salt
2 tablespoons lemon juice

Combine all the ingredients in a bowl and mix until well blended.

Serves 6 to 8.

Vegetables

Stuffed Tomatoes

Rice-Stuffed Tomatoes

Fried Red Tomatoes

Tomato Quiche Pie

Spinach Quiche

Fried Eggplant

Fried Green Tomato and Okra Patties

Fried Zucchini Squash

Green Beans and Corn

Green Beans with New Potatoes

Green Beans with Red Potatoes

Mixed Greens (Collards and Cabbage)

Swiss Chard Greens

Mixed Greens and Onions

Turnip with Kraut

Cauliflower

Mixed Summer Squash

Carrots, Celery, Onions, and Raisins

Candied Carrots	Mashed Potatoes with Garlic
Fresh Peas and Corn	and Sour Cream
Rutabagas and White Potatoes	Oven-Fried Potatoes
Country Collard Greens	Stuffed Baked Potato
Creamed Green Peas	Scalloped Potatoes
and Onions	Potatoes au Gratin
Creamy Corn Pudding	Bumpy Mashed Potato
Mexican Corn Pudding	Casserole
Buttered Silver Corn	Layered Zucchini Casserole
Orange-Stuffed Yams	Potato Casserole
Sweet Potatoes with Pineapple	Potato and Bacon Casserole
Sweet Potato Casserole	Broccoli and Potato Casserole
Yam and Banana Casserole	Corn and Cheese Casserole
German Potato Salad	Noodle and Vegetable Casserole

Cabbage Casserole

Broccoli and Rice Casserole

String Bean and Corn
    Casserole

Spanish Rice Casserole

Spanish Rice with Turkey
    Sausage

Sautéed Mixed Vegetables
    with Pasta

Mexican Baked Beans

Crock Pot Pinto Beans

Baked Great Northern Beans

Beans and Rice

Spanish Rice

Dirty Rice

Dirty Seasoned Rice

Peas, Mushrooms, and
    Rice Bowl

Spinach with Rice

Community Nurse Macaroni
    and Cheese

Quick Macaroni Dish

Macaroni and Tomatoes

Baked Apples

Fried Bananas

Baked Bananas

Stuffed Tomatoes

6 firm ripe tomatoes
1 pound lean ground turkey
2 tablespoons vegetable oil
3 tablespoons finely chopped
    onions
1 cup finely chopped celery

1 ½ cups cooked rice
1 ½ teaspoons dried basil,
    finely chopped
1 cup chopped tomatoes
4 tablespoons Parmesan cheese

Preheat oven to 350°. Cut the tops off the tomatoes and save them in the refrigerator for salad. Squeeze or scoop out the tomato seeds and reserve the juice. Sprinkle the insides with salt and invert the tomatoes to drain. Brown the turkey, drain the fat, and set aside. Heat the oil and sauté the onions and celery until done. Do not brown. Combine the turkey, rice, basil, chopped tomatoes, and reserved tomato juice. Stuff the whole tomatoes with the mixture. Place them on a shallow, oiled baking pan and sprinkle with the cheese. Bake for 50 minutes or until the tomatoes are soft but still firm. Serve hot.

Serves 6.

Rice-Stuffed Tomatoes

6 large firm ripe tomatoes
3 tablespoons butter or margarine
½ cup chopped onion
½ cup chopped green pepper
¼ cup chopped celery

½ cup uncooked rice,
prepared as directed
1 teaspoon garlic salt
black pepper to taste

Preheat oven to 350°. Slice a half inch from the top of the tomatoes and scoop out the pulp with a spoon. Put the pulp in a strainer to drain. Sprinkle some salt inside the tomatoes. Heat the butter in a pan and cook the onion, peppers, and celery until tender. Add the tomato pulp and rice. Add the garlic salt and pepper. Stuff the tomatoes with the rice mixture and place in a greased baking dish. Bake for 30 minutes or until done.

Serves 6.

Fried Red Tomatoes

Serve for a breakfast treat with hash browns and spring onions.

5 medium firm ripe tomatoes
1 cup buttermilk
1 egg, beaten
1 ½ cups self-rising flour

1 cup fine bread crumbs
1 teaspoon salt
½ pound bacon
½ cup vegetable oil

Slice the tomatoes ½ inch thick. Mix the buttermilk with the egg in a bowl and set aside. Stir the flour, bread crumbs, and salt together and set aside. Fry the bacon until crisp. Add the oil to the bacon drippings and heat on medium high. Dip the tomato slices in the buttermilk and egg and then coat with the flour mixture. Fry the tomato slices until brown on both sides. Place on paper towels to drain. Crumble on the bacon. Serve warm.

Serves 6.

Tomato Quiche Pie

2 tablespoons vegetable oil
1 stick butter or margarine
½ cup chopped onion
½ cup chopped green pepper
1 teaspoon garlic salt
½ teaspoon black pepper
2 pounds firm ripe tomatoes,
  chopped and seeded
1 teaspoon dried basil

3 eggs, beaten
3 tablespoons tomato paste
1 tablespoon cornstarch
1 9-inch pie shell, baked at 375°
  for 10 minutes
1 cup shredded Parmesan cheese
6 slices bacon, fried crisp and
  crumbled
½ cup sliced black olives

Preheat oven to 350°. Heat the oil and butter in a heavy skillet over
medium high and sauté the onion, green pepper, garlic salt, and black
pepper. Add the tomatoes and basil. Cover and cook over low heat for
5 minutes. Uncover and raise the heat so that the liquid evaporates. Do
not let the mixture scorch. Remove from the heat. Put the eggs and
tomato paste in a bowl and mix well; add to tomato mixture. Combine
the tomato mixture with the cornstarch and pour into the piecrust.
Top with the Parmesan cheese. Bake until firm and brown, about 30
minutes. Sprinkle with bacon and olives.

Serves 4.

Spinach Quiche

1 box (10 ounces) frozen chopped
    spinach, cooked and drained
4 ounces Swiss cheese
¼ cup chopped onion
1 9-inch pie shell, baked at 400°
    for 10 minutes

4 eggs, well beaten
1 cup milk
1 teaspoon garlic salt
1 teaspoon black pepper

Preheat oven to 350°. Mix together the spinach, cheese, and onion and spread in the pie shell. Combine the eggs, milk, salt, and pepper and pour over the spinach. Bake for 55 minutes. Let cool before slicing.

Serves 6 to 8.

Fried Eggplant

2 eggs, beaten
1½ cups milk
1½ cups self-rising flour
1 cup bread crumbs
1 teaspoon salt

½ teaspoon black pepper
2 medium eggplants, peeled and
    sliced into 1-inch rounds
Parmesan cheese (optional)
vegetable oil for frying

In a bowl, beat the eggs with the milk. Combine the flour, bread crumbs, salt, and pepper. Dip the eggplant slices into the milk mixture and then into the flour mixture to coat. Fry the eggplant in oil until brown on both sides. Don't overcrowd the skillet while frying. Drain on paper towels. Sprinkle with Parmesan cheese while hot.

Serves 6.

Fried Green Tomato and Okra Patties

½ pound fresh okra
2 large firm green tomatoes
¼ cup milk
1 egg, beaten

1 cup self-rising flour
4 tablespoons cornmeal
1 teaspoon salt
3 tablespoons vegetable oil

Slice the okra and dice the tomatoes. Set aside. In a bowl, beat together the milk and egg. In another bowl, stir together the flour, cornmeal, and salt. Heat the oil over medium high heat. Coat the okra and tomato pieces in the milk mixture and drain. Coat with the flour mixture and shake off excess. Put the okra and tomato into the hot oil. Press down with a spatula and let brown slowly. Put a plate over the top and turn the okra and tomato onto it, then slide back into the pan to brown on the other side. Remove from the oil and place on a paper towel–lined pan to drain.

Serves 6.

Fried Zucchini Squash

¾ cup milk
2 eggs, beaten
1 ½ cups self-rising flour
½ teaspoon black pepper

1 teaspoon salt
2 medium zucchini squash
vegetable oil for frying

Mix together the milk and eggs. Mix the self-rising flour with the pepper and salt. Slice the zucchini lengthwise into ¼ strips. Heat 3 inches of oil in a frying pan over medium high heat. Dip the zucchini in the milk wash, then in the flour mixture. Fry until brown. Do not crowd the frying pan. Drain the zucchini on paper towels and then put on a baking sheet. Keep in a warm oven until ready to serve.

Serves 4 to 6.

Green Beans and Corn

Whether you call them string, green, or snap beans, they are all the same. Use yellow or white corn and do not scrape the cob. Buy ready-sliced country side meat or use half a stick of butter or margarine.

2 slices pork streak of lean

4 cups water

1 teaspoon salt

1 teaspoon sugar (optional)

1½ pounds green beans, trimmed

3 ears corn, cut from the cob

Wash the meat and put it in a pot with water. Bring to a boil, then reduce the heat to medium and let cook for 25 minutes. Add the salt, sugar, and beans. Increase the heat to medium high and bring to a boil. Reduce the heat to medium low and let cook 35 to 40 minutes. Take out the meat and check the beans for tenderness. Stir in the corn and let cook slowly for 15 minutes.

Serves 6.

Green Beans with New Potatoes

1 can (14½ ounces) chicken broth + 1 can water

½ stick butter or margarine

1 teaspoon garlic salt

2 pounds fresh green beans, trimmed and cut into ½-inch pieces

1½ pounds small new potatoes

Put the broth, water, butter, and garlic salt in a pot and bring to a boil. Add the beans, then reduce the heat and cook for 25 minutes, stirring occasionally. Add the potatoes and cook until tender, about 20 minutes.

Serves 6.

Green Beans with Red Potatoes

1 slice streak of lean fatback
4 cups water
salt and black pepper to taste

2 pounds fresh green beans, trimmed
2 pounds red potatoes, cut in half

Wash the meat and put it into a pot with the water, salt, and pepper. Let come to a boil and reduce the heat to medium. Let cook slowly for 25 minutes. Add the green beans and cook for 25 minutes. Add the potatoes and cook until tender. Add more water if needed.

Serves 6 to 8.

Mixed Greens (Collards and Cabbage)

This is a good greens dish if you like milder collards. It is also good the next day.

3 slices country sidemeat
2 tablespoons vegetable oil
4 cups hot water
1 teaspoon sugar (optional)
2 teaspoons salt

3 pounds collard greens, shredded, large stems removed
1½ pounds cabbage, shredded
¼ teaspoon crushed red pepper (optional)

Wash the meat and add it with the oil to a large pot set over medium heat. Let cook slowly until done on both sides. Add the hot water and bring to a boil for 15 minutes. Remove the meat and add the sugar, salt, and collards; lower the heat and simmer for 40 minutes. Add the cabbage and stir to mix well. Add the red pepper, if desired. Cover and cook until tender, about 25 minutes. Mash a collard stem to check for tenderness. Add a little more hot water if needed.

Serves 6 to 8.

Swiss Chard Greens

Swiss chard is quick cooked like spinach, but it has large stems. It's best to cut them out, slice them into 1-inch pieces, and let them cook for 10 minutes before putting in the leaves. Like spinach, Swiss chard takes little water, but turn it to cook evenly.

1 can (14½ ounces) low-sodium
   chicken broth
¼ cup water

2½ pounds Swiss chard
½ stick butter or margarine
½ teaspoon garlic salt

Heat the broth and water to boiling. Stir in the chard stems, turn the heat to medium, and let cook for about 10 minutes. Then stir in the chard leaves to cook evenly, checking for tenderness after about 15 minutes. Do not drain, but stir in the butter and garlic salt. Use the pot liquor for dunking cornbread.

Serves 6.

Mixed Greens and Onions

Any kind of greens can be seasoned with onions. Turnip, kale, and mustard all cook in a similar manner.

1 ½ pounds turnip greens
1 pound mustard greens
1 pound kale
6 cups water

¾ stick butter or margarine
1 cup chopped onion
1 teaspoon salt

Wash the greens in cold water and remove the stems, then shred the leaves. Put the greens in a pot and cover with water. Cook slowly until tender. Heat the butter in a skillet over medium heat. Add the onion and sauté 3 to 4 minutes. Stir in the greens and let simmer 20 minutes. Add the salt.

Serves 6.

Turnip with Kraut

Miss Liza Snipes always made turnip kraut in a stone jar that sat in a corner beside the pie cabinet. I don't remember any other person who made this. I really loved it. This is close to the taste. Serve with pork or fish as a side dish. It used to be cooked in salt pork drippings and is good with fried dog bread patties.

3 tablespoons bacon drippings
2 cans (14½ ounces each)
  sauerkraut, drained

4 cups diced turnip
½ teaspoon crushed red pepper
salt to taste

Warm the bacon drippings in a pot on low heat. Add the sauerkraut, turnips, and red pepper. Add water to cover the vegetables by about 1 inch. Bring to a boil, then reduce the heat to low. Cook slowly, stirring to mix, about 45 minutes. Mash the turnips with a potato masher and salt to taste.

Serves 6 to 8.

Cauliflower

1 large head cauliflower
  (2–3 pounds)
1 can (10½ ounces) cream of
  mushroom soup

¼ cup milk
½ pound Velveeta cheese
2 hard-boiled eggs, grated or
  sliced

Preheat oven to 325°. Cut the cauliflower into small pieces. Cook in boiling salted water until just tender, about 12 minutes. Drain well and then put in a baking dish. Heat the soup and milk in a pot and stir in the cheese until it melts. Pour over the cauliflower. Bake until just bubbly. When ready to serve, spread the eggs over the top.

Serves 5.

Mixed Summer Squash

1 tablespoon vegetable oil
2 tablespoons butter
1 cup chopped onion
3 medium zucchini squash,
  washed and thinly sliced
4 medium yellow squash,
  washed and thinly sliced

1 teaspoon garlic salt
1 teaspoon dried dill
2 tablespoons grated Parmesan
  cheese

Heat the oil and butter in a skillet on medium heat. Sauté the onion until tender but not brown, about 5 to 6 minutes. Add the squash and sprinkle with the garlic salt and dill. Let cook until just tender. Serve over pasta and sprinkle with Parmesan cheese.

Serves 6.

Carrots, Celery, Onions, and Raisins

1 can (14½ ounces) chicken broth
  (add water to make 2 cups)
4 medium carrots, peeled and cut
  into ½-inch pieces
3 stalks celery, sliced into ½-inch
  pieces

2 tablespoons butter or margarine
1 jar (12 ounces) pearl onions
1 cup raisins
½ teaspoon dried dill
2 tablespoons cornstarch
2 tablespoons water

Heat the chicken broth in a pot until hot. Add the carrots. Cover the pot, reduce the heat to low, and let simmer for 15 minutes. Add the celery and let simmer until just tender, about 15 minutes. Drain off some of the liquid, if necessary. Add the butter, onions, raisins, and dill. Mix the cornstarch with the water and stir in. Turn off the heat, cover, and let ripen 10 to 12 minutes. Serve hot or cold.

Serves 6.

Candied Carrots

2 pounds carrots
½ cup brown sugar
½ teaspoon ginger
½ teaspoon salt

1 tablespoon cornstarch
1 cup orange juice
½ stick butter or margarine,
   melted

Peel and slice the carrots about ½ inch thick. Put them in a pot of water and cook until just tender, then drain. Mix the brown sugar, ginger, salt, cornstarch, and orange juice and set aside. Stir the butter into the carrots. Spread the brown sugar mixture over the carrots. Cover and let simmer on the stove for 20 minutes.

Serves 6.

Fresh Peas and Corn

Vegetables were often mixed together in country cooking. Early or late in the growing season there wasn't usually enough of one vegetable for the whole family. Find purple hull or black-eyed peas at the market. You can buy them shelled or in the hull. (You'll need about 3 pounds if you get them in the hull.)

3 cups black-eyed or purple
    hull peas
1 teaspoon salt
1 teaspoon sugar
½ stick butter or margarine or
    2 tablespoons bacon drippings

4 ears of fresh corn, cut from
    the cob
1 tablespoon flour

Wash the peas and skim off any loose skins or bad peas. Put the peas in a pot with enough hot water to cover them by 1 inch. Add the salt and sugar. Let come to a boil, reduce heat to medium low, and let cook until tender, about 35 minutes. Add the butter or bacon drippings to the pot. Stir in the corn and flour. Cook slowly for 15 to 20 minutes, adding a little water if needed.

Serves 6 to 8.

Rutabagas and White Potatoes

I like to use medium-sized rutabagas and potatoes.

1½–2 pounds rutabagas   1 teaspoon salt

1 pound baking potatoes   ½ cup milk

¾ stick butter or margarine

Peel and slice the rutabagas and potatoes. Put in a pot and cover with hot water. Let boil 25 minutes until tender. Drain, add the butter and salt, and mash. Pour in the milk and mix well by hand or with a mixer. Add more butter and milk if needed.

Serves 6 to 8.

Country Collard Greens

If you want to make this a vegetarian dish, use soy-based ham. Or eliminate the ham altogether and replace it with margarine.

1 pound country ham hock	½ teaspoon sugar
1½ quarts water	pinch crushed red pepper
2½–3 pounds collard greens	salt to taste

Wash the ham hock with warm water. Put it in a large pot with the water and bring to a boil; reduce the heat to low and cook for 1½ hours. Separate the collard leaves and cut off the large stems. Wash thoroughly. Roll up 2 to 3 leaves at a time and slice about ⅛ inch thick. Repeat until all the leaves are cut. Add to the pot, adding more hot water if necessary. Raise the heat and let the water come to a boil for a few minutes. Stir the pot, then cover it and reduce the heat to cook slowly until the greens are tender, about 1 hour. Add a little water if needed. Only a small amount of liquid should remain when done. Stir in the sugar, pepper, and salt. If using margarine instead of ham, cook the greens until tender, then drain them and add ¾ stick margarine, salt, and a pinch of sugar.

Serves 6 to 8.

Creamed Green Peas and Onions

This is a holiday side dish from a long time ago.

1 box (10 ounces) frozen small
   green peas, rinsed under cold
   water and drained
1 jar (12 ounces) cooked pearl
   onions, drained
2 tablespoons butter

1 cup chicken broth
½ cup evaporated milk
1 teaspoon sugar (optional)
1 tablespoon cornstarch
2 tablespoons water
salt and black pepper to taste

Put the peas and onions in a pot with the butter, broth, and evaporated milk and cook over medium heat for 15 minutes. Add the sugar, if desired. Mix the cornstarch with the water and add to the pot. Add the salt and pepper. Reduce the heat and simmer for 10 to 12 minutes.

Serves 6.

Creamy Corn Pudding

This was one of our favorite summertime dishes in the country. We loved to make it with fresh corn.

1½ cups milk
3 eggs, beaten
½ stick butter or margarine,
   melted

2 cups cream style corn
1 tablespoon flour
1 tablespoon sugar
1 teaspoon salt

Preheat oven to 350°. In a bowl, mix the milk, eggs, and butter, then stir in the corn. Combine the flour, sugar, and salt and add it to the corn mixture. Pour into a greased 1½-quart baking dish and bake for about 1 hour.

Serves 6.

Mexican Corn Pudding

1 tablespoon flour

1 tablespoon sugar

1 teaspoon salt

2 boxes (10 ounces each) frozen
cream style corn or 2 cans
(12 ounces each) cream corn

2 large eggs, beaten

2 tablespoons butter, melted

1 cup milk

1 small jar salsa con queso sauce
(taco dip)

½ cup Ritz cracker crumbs

Preheat oven to 350°. Mix the flour, sugar, and salt together. Stir in the corn and mix well. Add the eggs, and stir in the butter, milk, and salsa. Put the mixture in a greased 9 × 12 × 2-inch dish, and sprinkle the cracker crumbs on top. Bake for 50 minutes or until firm.

Serves 6 to 8.

Buttered Silver Corn

6–8 ears silver corn, shucked

½ stick butter

pinch sugar

1 teaspoon salt

¼ cup water

Cut the corn kernels from the cob. Melt the butter in a skillet on medium low heat and add the corn. Add the sugar and salt. Cook, stirring, for 8 to 10 minutes. Add the water; cover the skillet and simmer for 10 minutes.

Serves 6.

Orange-Stuffed Yams

This is a dish that I cooked on my first job and wrote about in my first book. After reading about it, my customers asked me, "Why didn't you put the recipe in the first book?" Here it is.

6 large oranges
1 can mashed sweet potatoes (yams)
1 cup packed light brown sugar
½ stick + 1 tablespoon butter
2 eggs, beaten
¼ cup milk

pinch salt
¼ teaspoon ginger
½ teaspoon nutmeg
½ teaspoon cinnamon
¼ cup crushed pecan pieces

Preheat oven to 350°. Cut the oranges in half, remove the pulp, and place on a baking pan. Removing a small slice from the bottom of the orange will allow it to sit up straight on the pan. Mash the sweet potatoes in a bowl and mix in ¾ cup of the brown sugar, ½ stick butter, eggs, milk, salt, and spices. Spoon the yam mixture into the orange halves and bake for 40 minutes.

To make a topping, mix 1 tablespoon of the butter with ¼ brown sugar and the pecan pieces. Spread on top of the yam mixture.

Serves 6.

Sweet Potatoes with Pineapple

3 pounds sweet potatoes
1 can (15¼ ounces) sliced pineapple
1 cup brown sugar
1 tablespoon cornstarch

½ stick butter, melted
1 cup orange juice
pinch salt

Preheat oven to 375°. Select sweet potatoes near the same size. Cook the potatoes covered with water until fork tender, 20 to 30 minutes depending on size. Drain and cool. Peel and slice the potatoes about 1 inch thick. Overlap the potatoes in a baking dish and put the pineapple on top. Mix together the brown sugar, cornstarch, butter, orange juice, and salt. Spread over the potatoes and pineapples. Cover and bake for 35 to 40 minutes until the sweet potatoes are tender.

Serves 8.

Sweet Potato Casserole

1 can (16 ounces) mashed
    sweet potatoes
1 cup brown sugar
¼ stick butter, melted
1 egg, beaten
½ teaspoon ground cloves

½ cup evaporated milk
pinch salt
1 teaspoon nutmeg
1 package (10½ ounces) miniature
    marshmallows

Preheat oven to 375°. Mix all the ingredients except the marshmallows together and pour into a 1½-quart baking pan. Bake for 40 minutes, then spread the marshmallows over the top and bake until they are golden brown.

Serves 6.

Yam and Banana Casserole

Every year one of the family members brings a new dish to our reunion. This is one of the favorites on my mother's side of the family.

2 ½ pounds medium yams

2 firm ripe bananas, sprinkled
   with a small amount of lemon
   juice

½ cup corn syrup

2 cups water

½ stick butter or margarine

1 cup brown sugar

1 teaspoon salt

½ teaspoon cinnamon

Put the yams in a large pot, cover with water, and bring to a boil. Reduce the heat to medium. Let the yams cook until fork tender, about 30 minutes. Drain and pour cold water over them. When cool, peel and cut into 1-inch slices. Put in a casserole dish and slice the bananas a ½ inch thick over the top. In a saucepan set over medium heat, mix the corn syrup and water, then add the butter, sugar, salt, and cinnamon. Pour the sauce over the yams and bananas and bake on a lower rack of the oven at 350° degrees for 30 to 40 minutes.

Serves 6.

German Potato Salad

This potato salad can be served hot with roast pork.

2 pounds small new potatoes

6 strips bacon, cooked until crisp, drain

1 cup chopped onion, cooked in bacon fat

1 cup chicken broth

3 tablespoons cider vinegar

1 teaspoon celery seed

salt and black pepper to taste

Put the potatoes in a pot and cover them with hot water. Bring the water to a boil and cook the potatoes for 25 to 30 minutes; then drain, cool, and peel. Meanwhile, fry the bacon until crisp then set aside. Add the onion to the skillet and cook until tender, 3 to 4 minutes. Slice the potatoes, add them to the skillet, set aside. Heat the chicken broth and vinegar in a saucepan. Stir in the potatoes and onion. Add the celery seed, salt, and pepper. Crumble the bacon over and serve warm.

Serves 6 to 8.

Mashed Potatoes with Garlic and Sour Cream

2 pounds baking potatoes
½ stick butter
1 teaspoon garlic salt

½ cup sour cream
½ cup milk

Peel the potatoes and cut in half. Put them in a large pot and cover with water. Let boil until well done; drain. Beat the potatoes with a hand mixer and add the butter and garlic salt. Beat until mixed. Add the sour cream and milk, mixing until fluffy. Cover and keep over low heat until ready to serve.

Serves 6.

Oven-Fried Potatoes

3 large baking potatoes, scrubbed
⅛ cup vegetable oil
2 teaspoons seasoning salt

Preheat oven to 425°. Slice the potatoes lengthwise into ½-inch strips. Place the potatoes in cold water with a few ice cubes and let sit for about 1 hour. Drain and pat dry. Place the potatoes on a baking pan and brush them with the oil. Shake on the seasoning salt. Bake for 25 minutes, turning once, cooking until brown. Remove from the oven and shake on seasoning salt to taste.

Serves 4 to 6.

Stuffed Baked Potato

This is good for luncheons.

4 large baking potatoes

4 slices of bacon, cooked crisp
  (bake in the oven for best results)

4 ounces cream cheese

½ cup sour cream

¼ cup milk

2 tablespoons butter

2 tablespoons chopped chives

2 spring onions, chopped

salt to taste

Preheat oven to 400°. Wash and dry the potatoes and prick with a fork. Rub lightly with oil. Place the potatoes on a foil-lined baking sheet. Let bake 1 hour until done. Remove from oven and place on a rack. Let cool for 10 minutes. You will need an oven mitt or towel to handle the potatoes. With a steak knife, carefully cut the potatoes in half without breaking. Scoop out the potato flesh with a spoon and place the potato skins on a baking sheet. Mix together the potato pulp with the other ingredients and spoon into the potato skins. Bake for 12 to 15 minutes.

Makes 8 halves.

Scalloped Potatoes

3 tablespoons butter or margarine
½ cup finely chopped onion
2 tablespoons flour
1 large can (12 ounces)
    evaporated milk

1 cup chicken broth
2 pounds medium potatoes,
    peeled and cut into thin slices

Preheat oven to 375°. Heat the butter in a skillet and cook the onion until softened but not brown. Add the flour, evaporated milk, and broth, stirring until smooth. Put the potatoes in a baking dish and pour the milk mixture over the top. Cover and bake for 40 minutes until tender.

Serves 6.

Potatoes au Gratin

This is a dish that is gone but not forgotten!

2 pounds white potatoes
½ stick butter or margarine
1 cup milk

1 teaspoon salt
2 cups grated sharp cheddar cheese

Preheat oven to 350°. Wash and peel the potatoes. Put in a pot, cover with water, and boil until tender. Drain the potatoes and mash them with butter, milk, and salt. Stir to mix and then blend in half the cheese. Pour into a baking dish and spread with the remaining cheese. Bake for 20 minutes.

Serves 6.

Bumpy Mashed Potato Casserole

8 medium potatoes
1 teaspoon salt
1 package (8 ounces) cream cheese

2 eggs, beaten
1 tablespoon flour
2 tablespoons chopped chives

Peel the potatoes and cut into quarters. Cook, covered in water, for about 20 minutes until fork tender. Drain, add the salt and cream cheese, and mash. Blend in the eggs slowly and then add the flour and chives. Spoon into a buttered casserole dish and bake at 350° for 25 minutes until hot.

Serves 6 to 8.

Layered Zucchini Casserole

2 pounds zucchini
¼ cup chopped onion
¼ cup water
1 can (10½ ounces) chicken soup
1 cup sour cream

½ teaspoon salt
½ stick of butter
1 package (16 ounces) cornbread
    dressing mix

Wash and slice the zucchini and cook with the onion and water. Stir to cook evenly. Stir in the soup, sour cream, and salt when squash is tender. Combine the butter with the cornbread dressing mix. Put a layer of the cornbread dressing in the bottom of a baking dish and then top with a layer of the zucchini mixture. Continue to alternate layers, ending with a layer of the cornbread mixture. Bake at 350° for 30 minutes.

Serves 6 to 8.

Potato Casserole

1 ½ pounds potatoes, peeled
and sliced
1 can (14 ½ ounces) chicken broth
1 ½ cups milk

2 tablespoons cornstarch
1 cup shredded cheese
2 cups buttered cracker crumbs

Preheat oven to 350°. Place the sliced potatoes in a pot. Add water just to cover. Cook for 15 minutes. Drain the potatoes and pour into a baking dish. Set aside. Heat the broth and milk in a pot. When hot, stir in the cornstarch. Stir in the cheese and pour the mixture over the potatoes. Spread with cracker crumbs. Bake about 40 minutes.

Serves 6 to 8.

Potato and Bacon Casserole

2 pounds white potatoes, peeled,
cooked, and drained
2 tablespoons butter

1 cup cheddar cheese, grated
1 cup sour cream
6 slices bacon, cooked until crisp

Preheat oven to 375°. Beat the potatoes with a hand mixer and add the butter, cheese, and sour cream; blend well. Pour into a greased 2-quart casserole dish and bake for 30 minutes. Remove from the oven and crumble the bacon over the top. Turn off the heat and return the casserole to the off oven, letting it set for 10 minutes.

Serves 6 to 8.

Broccoli and Potato Casserole

1 large package (16 ounces)
   frozen cut broccoli, thawed
1 can (14½ ounces) chicken broth
1 tablespoon cornstarch
2 tablespoons water

¼ stick of butter
1 jar (8 ounces) Cheese Whiz
1 can (16 ounces) whole white
   potatoes, drained, rinsed,
   and sliced

Preheat oven to 350°. Squeeze the water from the broccoli and set aside. Heat the chicken broth in a pot. Combine the cornstarch with the water and add to the broth. Reduce the heat to low and add the butter and Cheese Whiz, stirring to melt. Layer the broccoli and potatoes in a baking dish. Pour the broth mixture over the top and bake for 50 minutes until bubbling hot. Check the broccoli for tenderness. Do not over bake.

Serves 6.

Corn and Cheese Casserole

2 tablespoons butter, melted

2 cups crushed saltine crackers

4 slices bacon

½ cup chopped spring onions

2 eggs, beaten

1 box (10 ounces) frozen cream corn,
    thawed, or 1 can (12 ounces) cream corn

1¼ cups milk

2 teaspoons sugar

1 cup grated cheddar cheese

½ teaspoon salt

Preheat oven to 350°. Combine the butter and 1 cup of the crackers and set aside. In a fry pan, cook the bacon until crisp. Remove the bacon from the pan and pour off all but 2 tablespoons of the drippings. Crumble the bacon when cool. Add the onions to the pan and cook until tender. Add the remaining cup of crackers to the pan, mix well, and turn off the heat. In a bowl, mix together all the remaining ingredients except the buttered crackers. Mix in the onion mixture and pour into a baking dish. Spread the buttered crackers on top. Bake for 40 to 50 minutes.

Serves 6.

Noodle and Vegetable Casserole

½ cup vegetable oil
½ cup chopped sweet onion
1 pound mushrooms, sliced
salt and black pepper to taste
½ teaspoon dried dill
1 can (10½ ounces) cream of
    mushroom soup

1 package (16 ounces) wide egg
    noodles, prepared as directed
3 medium zucchini squash, sliced
4 eggs, beaten
½ cup cracker crumbs

Preheat oven to 350°. Heat the oil in a skillet over medium heat, add the onion and mushrooms, and cook until done, 8 to 10 minutes. Add salt and pepper. Add the dill and soup. Stir in the noodles and squash; mix well. Let cool. Add the eggs and mix well. Pour into a large baking pan and sprinkle on the cracker crumbs. Bake for 45 minutes.

Serves 6.

Cabbage Casserole

This was my mother's family reunion casserole. A real treat!

1 medium cabbage, shredded
¼ cup water
1 cup milk
2 tablespoons butter or margarine
2 tablespoons flour

1 cup shredded cheddar cheese
1 teaspoon salt
pinch crushed red pepper
1 cup buttered cracker crumbs

Preheat oven to 375°. Bring the water to a boil and cook the cabbage in it for about 10 minutes; drain. Add the milk, butter, and flour to a saucepan, stirring to mix well. Cook until thickened. Stir in the cheese until melted. Add the cabbage, salt, and pepper. Pour into a greased casserole dish. Spread the buttered cracker crumbs over the dish. Bake for 20 to 25 minutes.

Serves 4 to 6.

Broccoli and Rice Casserole

This is another dish that we mixed together when I was growing up. Rice can be mixed with almost any vegetable to make a good meal.

1 can (14½ ounces) chicken broth
½ cup milk
2 tablespoons cornstarch
2 tablespoons water
1 jar (8 ounces) Cheese Whiz
2 teaspoons garlic salt

2 boxes (10 ounces each) frozen
    chopped broccoli, thawed
2 cups uncooked rice,
    prepared as directed
1 cup Ritz cracker crumbs,
    buttered

Preheat oven to 350°. Put the broth and milk in a pot on medium heat. Stir the cornstarch into the water and add to the pot. Stir in the Cheese Whiz and reduce the heat. Add the garlic salt and broccoli. Mix the broccoli mixture and rice together and pour into a baking dish. Bake for 25 minutes. Top with buttered cracker crumbs.

Serves 6 to 8.

String Bean and Corn Casserole

2 cans (14½ ounce each) French cut green beans
1 can (14½ ounces) yellow corn
1 can (10½ ounces) cream of mushroom soup
1 can (12 ounces) French fried onions

Rinse the green beans and corn under cold water, drain, and pour into a casserole dish. Pour the soup over the bean and corn mixture. Top with the onions. Bake at 350° for 30 minutes.

Serves 6.

Spanish Rice Casserole

3 tablespoons vegetable oil
½ cup chopped onion
¼ cup chopped green pepper
1 pound ground pork
2 tablespoons brown sugar

2 cans (14½ ounces each)
    stewed tomatoes
1 cup uncooked rice,
    prepared as directed

Heat the oil in a skillet, and sauté the onion and pepper about 3 minutes. Do not brown. Add the pork and sauté until brown. Add the sugar and tomatoes to the skillet. Stir in the rice. Let simmer 12 to 15 minutes.

Serves 6.

Spanish Rice with Turkey Sausage

1 cup sliced small onions
¼ cup chopped green pepper
¼ stick butter
1 pound turkey links, sliced
1 teaspoon brown sugar
1 cup uncooked rice,
    prepared as directed

2 cans (14½ ounces) stewed
    tomatoes
2 teaspoons dried basil
⅛ teaspoon hot pepper sauce

Preheat oven to 350°. Sauté the onion and pepper in the butter until softened but not brown. Add the sausage and cook for 10 minutes. Stir in the brown sugar, rice, tomatoes, basil, and hot pepper sauce. Pour into a casserole dish. Bake for about 30 minutes.

Serves 6.

Sautéed Mixed Vegetables with Pasta

½ pound asparagus
1 cup snow peas
½ stick butter or margarine
½ pound sliced mushrooms
1 medium red pepper, sliced
4 spring onions, chopped,
    including a little of the green

1 teaspoon garlic salt
1 box (16 ounces) spaghetti,
    prepared as directed
Parmesan cheese

Wash the asparagus, snap off the tough ends, and cut into 1½-inch pieces. Put the asparagus and snow peas in a colander over boiling water and cover. Let stand until hot. Remove and set aside. Heat the butter in a large pan. Stir in the mushrooms, peppers, and onions and sauté until tender. Add the garlic salt and stir in the asparagus and snow peas. Pour the noodles on a large platter and spoon the vegetables over them. Sprinkle with Parmesan cheese.

Serves 8.

Mexican Baked Beans

2 cans (15 ounces each) great
    northern beans, drained
1 cup ketchup
¼ cup brown sugar
1 cup hot salsa

1 can (4½ ounces) green
    chili peppers
1 tablespoon Worcestershire
    sauce
3 strips bacon

Preheat oven to 375°. Put the beans in a baking dish. Stir in the ketchup, brown sugar, salsa, and chili peppers. Add the Worcestershire sauce. Lay the bacon across the top. Bake for 45 minutes.

Serves 6.

Crock Pot Pinto Beans

You can use butter, margarine, or ham hock to season.

1 pound bag dried pinto beans
2 teaspoons garlic salt
½ cup chopped onion
ham hock, butter, or margarine

Wash the beans in warm water. Whisk to remove grit and then drain the beans. Put the beans in a small pot and boil for 20 minutes. Drain the beans and put in a crock pot with the garlic salt, onion, ham hock (or butter or margarine), and enough water to cover by 2 inches. Cook until the beans are tender, adding a little hot water if needed.

Serves 6.

Baked Great Northern Beans

¾ cup chopped onion
3 tablespoons bacon drippings
1 pound dried great northern
    beans, cooked as directed
1 cup ketchup
1 cup hot salsa
2 tablespoons vinegar
1 teaspoon mustard
¼ cup brown sugar

Preheat oven to 400°. Sauté the onion in the bacon drippings. Put the beans in a mixing bowl and add the onion and the remaining ingredients. Pour into a baking dish and cook for 45 minutes.

Serves 6.

Beans and Rice

In the country we grew up mixing a lot of foods together— like these vegetables.

2 tablespoons vegetable oil
2 medium onions, chopped fine
1 tablespoon minced garlic
¾ cup chopped celery
1 green pepper, seeded and
  chopped

¾ cup sundried tomatoes
1 can (14½ ounces) beef broth
1 can (15 ounces) black beans
2 cups uncooked rice,
  prepared as directed

In a large saucepan or electric skillet, heat the oil on medium heat and add the onion, garlic, and celery. Stir while cooking for 2 minutes. Add the pepper and let cook for 5 minutes, then add the tomatoes. Stir in the broth and beans and let come to a boil, then reduce the heat to simmer for 25 minutes. Stir in the rice.

Serves 6 to 8.

Spanish Rice

One of the older dishes that you see in fraternity and sorority houses on UNC's campus. I like to serve this with grilled pork chops.

¼ cup vegetable oil
1 cup chopped onion
½ cup chopped celery
1 cup chopped green pepper
2 cans (14 ounces each)
   stewed tomatoes

1 can (6 ounces) tomato paste
1½ cups uncooked rice,
   prepared as directed
2 teaspoons garlic salt
1 tablespoon chili powder
2 tablespoons brown sugar

Preheat oven to 350°. Heat the oil in a large fry pan over medium heat. Add the onion, celery, and green pepper. Cook, stirring, until tender, and set aside. Put the tomatoes and tomato paste in a pot and bring to a boil. Reduce the heat, and add the remaining ingredients, and simmer about 30 minutes. Pour into a baking dish and bake for 35 to 40 minutes.

Serves 6.

Dirty Rice

This recipe is for those who love liver!

¾ stick butter or margarine
1 pound liver pudding
2 tablespoons chopped onion

1 teaspoon crushed red pepper
1 cup uncooked rice,
   prepared as directed

In a skillet over medium high heat, melt the butter and then add the liver pudding. Stir to crumble with a potato masher. Add the onion and pepper and cook until hot. Stir in the rice.

Serves 8.

Dirty Seasoned Rice

½ pound chicken livers

1 can (10½ ounces) chicken broth

2 tablespoons vegetable oil

½ cup finely chopped sweet onion

2 tablespoons flour

1½ cups uncooked rice,
   prepared as directed

pinch crushed red pepper
   (optional)

Wash the livers and cut off the fat and tough parts. Cook the livers slowly in broth until done, 10 to 15 minutes. Cool and chop fine. Heat the oil in a skillet and sauté the onion; do not brown. Stir in the flour and mix well. Stir in the livers with the cooking liquid, rice, and red pepper. Cook slowly for 10 to 12 minutes. Rice should be moist.

Serves 6 to 8.

Peas, Mushrooms, and Rice Bowl

They serve this at the hospital all the time.

1 can (14½ ounces) chicken broth

1 box (10 ounces) frozen green peas

½ stick butter or margarine

1 can (4 ounces) sliced mushrooms, drained

1 cup rice, cooked as directed

Bring the broth to a boil in a pot. Put in the peas and let come to a boil; cover and simmer for 15 minutes. Add the butter, mushrooms, and rice. Let simmer until all is hot.

Serves 6.

Spinach with Rice

I suggest that you serve this with baked chicken— a good combination!

1 cup rice, prepared as directed
2 packages (10 ounces each) frozen chopped spinach,
    prepared as directed
1 teaspoon garlic salt

Mix the cooked rice with the spinach and garlic salt. Cover and simmer for 8 to 10 minutes to let ripen.

Serves 6.

Community Nurse
Macaroni and Cheese

In the 1950s the community nurse was the one who came around after you had your babies and made sure you had a healthy diet. This was when powdered milk became popular, and she taught us how to use it in different dishes. She made good macaroni and cheese. I had learned to use dry milk in main dishes in the 1940s.

1 cup dry milk
¼ cup flour
1 teaspoon salt
2 cups water
1 teaspoon Worcestershire sauce
½ pound shredded sharp cheese
½ stick butter or margarine,
    melted

2 eggs, beaten
1 box (16 ounces) elbow macaroni,
    prepared as directed
½ cup bread or cracker crumbs,
    buttered

Preheat oven to 375°. Mix together the first 8 ingredients in a big bowl. Stir in the macaroni and pour into a 1½-quart baking dish. Top with bread or cracker crumbs. Bake for 45 minutes.

Serves 6.

Quick Macaroni Dish

Unlike most macaroni and cheese dishes, this one has eggs in it.

½ stick butter or margarine
2 tablespoons flour
2 cups milk
1 block (12 ounces) Velveeta cheese

1 box (16 ounces) small elbow
    macaroni, prepared as directed
2 eggs, beaten

Preheat oven to 350°. Heat the butter in a pot over medium heat. Stir in the flour and milk. Cook until hot. Add the cheese to the milk mixture, stirring until cheese is melted. Stir in the macaroni. Add the eggs. Pour in a deep casserole dish and bake for about 25 minutes.

Serves 6 to 8.

Macaroni and Tomatoes

1 box (16 ounces) rigatoni, prepared as directed
2 cans (14½ ounces each) stewed tomatoes
½ stick butter or margarine, melted
salt and black pepper to taste
½ teaspoon dried basil

Prehead oven to 350°. Combine all the ingredients and place in a baking dish. Bake for about 30 minutes until hot.

Serves 8.

Baked Apples

This is a good side dish for any meal.

6 medium firm cooking apples
½ cup water
½ cup brown sugar

1 teaspoon cinnamon
2 tablespoons butter or margarine,
   melted

Preheat oven to 375°. Cut each apple into 8 slices. Remove the seeded area and cut out any dark spots. Put the apples in a 9 × 13 × 2-inch casserole dish. Mix together the water, brown sugar, cinnamon, and butter and pour over the apples. Cover and bake for 30 minutes, stirring after the first 15 minutes. Take from the oven and stir. The apples should be a little firm. Cover and serve warm.

Serves 6 to 8.

Fried Bananas

2 tablespoons sugar
¼ cup self-rising flour
1 tablespoon cornstarch
½ cup evaporated milk
1 egg, beaten

1 tablespoon melted butter
3 firm ripe bananas
2 cups vegetable oil for frying
powdered sugar

Mix together the sugar, flour, and cornstarch. Combine the evaporated milk, egg, and butter and stir in the flour mixture just until combined. Cut the bananas into 1-inch pieces and dip into the mixture to cover. Fry in hot oil until brown on all sides. Drain on paper towels and sprinkle with powdered sugar.

Serves 6.

Baked Bananas

This is good on waffles, pancakes, French toast, or ice cream— it can be used in so many ways.

6 medium firm bananas
½ cup brown sugar
½ stick butter, melted
1 teaspoon lemon juice

Preheat oven to 375°. Slice the bananas in half lengthwise and place in a baking dish. Mix together the brown sugar, butter, and lemon juice and spread over the bananas. Bake for 12 minutes.

Serves 6 to 8.

Cakes, Pies, and Other Desserts

Orange Cream Cheese Icing

Orange Cake Layers

Pineapple Cake

Apricot Upside-Down Cake

Peach Upside-Down Cake

Pineapple-Carrot-Raisin
　Layer Cake

Poppy Seed Cake

Pumpkin Tube Cake

Pumpkin Layer Cake

Banana-Pineapple-Nut Cake

Brown Sugar Pound Cake

Prune Pound Cake

Sour Cream Pound Cake

Old-Fashioned Lemon
　Pound Cake

Quick Lemon Pound Cake

Pineapple Filling

Lemon Filling

Lemon Curd

Chocolate Fudge Icing I

Chocolate Fudge Icing II

Cocoa Chocolate Icing

Cooked Chocolate Icing

White Chocolate Icing

Fluffy White Icing

Caramel Icing

Orange Icing

Buttercream Frosting

Cooked Butter Icing

Chocolate Pie

Mince Meat Pie

Chess Pie

Lemon Chess Pie

Chocolate Pie with
　Cookie Crust

Coconut Cream Pie

Coconut-Pineapple Pie

Chocolate Pecan Pie

Sweet Potato-Pecan-
　Coconut Pie

Lemon Meringue Pie

Old-Fashioned Apple Pie

Apple Pie Crumble

French Apple Pie

Easy Boston Cream Pie

Fresh Peach Pie

Sweet Potato–Pumpkin Pie

Sweet Potato–Coconut Pie

Sweet Potato Custard Pie

White Potato Pie

Cherry-Rhubarb Cobbler

Tomato Cobbler

Piecrust

Fresh Blackberry Dessert

Deep-Dish Apricot Dessert

Apple Brown Betty

Apple Bread Pudding

Coconut Bread Pudding

Egg Noodle Pudding

Chocolate Bread Pudding

Dessert Waffles with Ice Cream
    and Chocolate

Butterscotch Cookies

Apple-Nut Squares

Coconut Squares

Brownies with Macadamia
    Nuts

Baked Fudge

Heavenly Hash

Ice Box Dessert

Banana Split Dessert

Peach Dessert

Vanilla Milkshake

Chocolate-Dipped Fruit

Friendship Cake

Tips on Baking Cakes

When baking a cake, all the ingredients should be at room temperature. Pull all the ingredients together prior to baking, measure them, and add them in the order in which they appear in the recipe. Grease and flour the pans prior to putting together the recipe. You can use either an 8-inch or 9-inch pan. If you use an 8-inch pan, the cake will have thicker layers. After baking, always let the cake sit in the pan for 10 minutes, then remove and let cool on rack.

White Fruitcake

This is an old recipe— at least 50 years old—from the late Alice Parsley's collection and was sent to me by mail.

2 cups all-purpose flour
1 teaspoon baking powder
2 teaspoons nutmeg
½ pound butter, softened
2 cups sugar
6 eggs
5 tablespoons white sherry, wine, or orange juice
½ pound candied pineapple

½ pound citron
1 pound candied cherries
1 pound box golden raisins
½ pound almonds
½ pound walnuts
½ pound pecans
1 small coconut, grated by hand, or 1 package (6 ounces) frozen coconut

Preheat oven to 250°. Combine the flour, baking powder, and nutmeg and set aside. Cream the butter and sugar very thoroughly. Add the eggs one at a time, beating well after each addition. Add the sherry. Fold in the dry mixture. Chop the fruit and nuts and toss in a little flour. Stir into the batter and mix well. Add the coconut. Line a greased pound cake pan with wax paper and pour the batter into the pan. Bake for 3 hours. Cool overnight. Remove and wrap in a wine and brandy soaked cheesecloth, and store the cake in a cool place.

Serves 12.

A 1939 Country Wedding Cake

This cake was put together in a big bowl and mixed with a wooden spoon.

3 sticks butter

¼ cup Crisco

4 cups sugar

10 large eggs

4 cups all-purpose flour

1 teaspoon vanilla extract

2 teaspoons lemon extract

½ teaspoon mace

Preheat oven to 325°. Beat the butter and Crisco with an electric mixer on medium until fluffy. Add the sugar a little at a time, beating until light and fluffy. Add the eggs one at a time, beating until the yolks are well blended. Reduce the speed to low and add the flour, 1 cup at a time. Add the vanilla, lemon extract, and mace. Stir, scraping down the batter from the side of the bowl until well blended. Do not overmix. Pour the batter into a 10-inch tube pan and bake for 1 hour and 40 minutes.

Serves 10 to 12.

Norma's Wedding Cake Top

3 sticks butter, softened

1 box (1 pound) powdered sugar

6 eggs

3 cups all-purpose flour

½ teaspoon mace

½ teaspoon nutmeg

2 teaspoons lemon juice

Preheat oven to 325°. Beat the butter on medium and until fluffy. Add the powdered sugar in thirds, beating after each addition. Add the eggs one at a time, and beat well after adding each. In a bowl, mix the flour, mace, and nutmeg. Add to the batter in thirds and then add lemon juice. Scrape down the sides of the bowl. Mix quickly until blended. Pour into a greased and floured tube pan and bake for 1 hour and 10 minutes.

Serves 10 to 12.

Red Velvet Cake

1 cup butter
2 cups sugar
2 eggs, beaten
1 tablespoon vinegar
1 tablespoon cocoa
3 tablespoons red food coloring

2½ cups all-purpose flour
1½ teaspoons baking soda
½ teaspoon salt
1 cup buttermilk
1 teaspoon vanilla extract

Frosting

1 stick butter or margarine,
  softened
1 package (8 ounces)
  cream cheese, softened

1 box (1 pound) powdered sugar
1 teaspoon vanilla extract
1 cup chopped walnuts

Preheat oven to 350°. Cream the butter, sugar, eggs, vinegar, cocoa, and food coloring and beat well. Combine the flour, soda, and salt in a separate bowl. Add the buttermilk and vanilla to the cream mixture. Add the flour mixture. Beat until well mixed. Pour into 3 9-inch greased and floured baking pans and bake for 20 minutes.

For the frosting, blend together all the ingredients except the nuts. Ice each layer and top the cake with nuts.

Serves 10.

Aunt Laura's Strawberry Jelly Cake

We would walk miles in search of wild strawberries.

2 tablespoons all-purpose flour
1 box yellow cake mix
2 packages (10 ounces each)
   frozen strawberries

1 tablespoon lemon juice
1 cup sugar
2 tablespoons cornstarch
2 tablespoons water

Preheat oven to 350°. Add the flour to the cake mix and prepare the batter as directed on the package. Pour the batter into 2 greased and floured 9-inch baking pans and bake for 25 minutes. Mix together the strawberries, lemon juice, and 3 tablespoons of the sugar in a pot. Bring to a boil. Stir in the cornstarch and water. Let set on the counter overnight. Pour the strawberries into a pot and stir in the rest of the sugar. Boil about 10 minutes. Cool and spread over cake layers while warm. Prick holes in the cake with a toothpick to allow the syrup to seep in and mellow.

Serves 8 to 10.

Chocolate Layer Cake

2 sticks unsalted butter, softened
¼ cup shortening
2½ cups sugar
5 large eggs
2 teaspoons vanilla extract

3 cups all-purpose flour
¼ teaspoon salt
2 teaspoons baking powder
1 cup milk

Chocolate Icing

4 squares unsweetened chocolate
1 stick butter
1½ boxes powdered sugar,
   sifted if lumpy

1 teaspoon vanilla extract
3–4 tablespoons milk

Preheat oven to 350°. In a mixing bowl, cream the butter and shortening. Add the sugar and beat until fluffy. Add the eggs one at a time and mix for about a minute after each addition. Add the vanilla. In a separate bowl, sift the flour, salt, and baking powder. Add the flour half a cup at a time and blend together well after each addition. Add the milk and blend. Do not overmix. Pour into 3 greased and floured 9-inch baking pans and bake for 25 minutes or until done.

To make the icing, melt the chocolate and butter in the top of a double boiler or in the microwave, covered. Put the sugar in a bowl and pour in the chocolate mixture. Stir to mix. Add the vanilla. Add the milk a little at a time and beat until smooth. Thin with more milk if necessary.

Serves 10 to 12.

Chocolate Fudge Cake

1 cup semisweet chocolate chips
½ cup chocolate syrup
1 pound butter, softened
1 tablespoon vegetable
   shortening
2½ cups sugar

4 eggs
1 cup buttermilk,
   at room temperature
1 teaspoon baking soda
3 cups flour
2 teaspoons vanilla extract

Preheat oven to 300°. Melt the chocolate chips in a saucepan with the chocolate syrup. Set aside. Cream the butter and shortening in a large mixing bowl. Slowly add the sugar, continuing to beat on medium speed. Add the eggs one at a time, beating well after each addition. Pour the chocolate mixture and buttermilk into another bowl and stir in the baking soda. Mix well, then add by thirds to the cream mixture, alternating with the flour. Stir with a wooden spoon until blended; do not over beat. Stir in the vanilla. Pour into a well-greased 10-inch tube pan and bake for 1½ hours. Let cool and remove from the pan onto a cake plate. Sprinkle with powered sugar or icing.

Serves 10 to 12.

Dark Chocolate Stack Cake

2 sticks butter, softened

2 cups sugar

3 large eggs

2½ cups self-rising flour

¼ cup cornstarch

1 teaspoon baking powder

¾ cup milk

1 teaspoon vanilla extract

Preheat oven to 350°. In a mixing bowl, cream the butter and sugar. Add one egg at a time, beating after each addition. Combine the flour, cornstarch, and baking powder. Stir in the flour mixture in thirds, alternating with the milk, until blended. Add the vanilla. Bake in 3 9-inch greased and floured pans. Bake for 25 to 30 minutes, then check for doneness. Let cool over night. With a sharp knife, cut each layer in half. Frost the layers with chocolate icing.

Serves 8 to 10.

German Chocolate Cake

1 cup Crisco shortening

2 cups sugar

4 eggs, separated

1 teaspoon vanilla extract

1 package (10 ounces) German
   chocolate, melted

2½ cups sifted all-purpose flour

1 teaspoon baking soda

½ teaspoon salt

1 cup buttermilk

Preheat oven to 350°. Cream the shortening and sugar until light.
Add the egg yolks one at a time. Mix well after each addition. Add
the vanilla and melted chocolate and mix until smooth. Sift the flour,
baking soda, and salt together. Alternate adding the buttermilk and
the flour mixture by thirds, mixing until smooth. Whip the egg whites
until lightly stiff and fold them in. Pour the batter evenly into 3 well-
greased and floured (or paper-lined) 9-inch baking pans. Bake for 35 to
40 minutes. Cool and frost with German Chocolate Frosting (see the
following recipe).

Serves 12.

German Chocolate Frosting

1 large can (12 ounces)
   evaporated milk
3 egg yolks
1 stick butter, softened
1 ½ cups sugar

pinch salt (to keep from sticking
   and to cool quicker)
1 teaspoon vanilla extract
1 cup coconut
1 cup chopped nuts

Put 2 tablespoons of the evaporated milk in the egg yolks and beat. Set aside. Add the butter, sugar, and remaining evaporated milk and salt to a saucepan, stirring to mix well. Cook over medium heat until lukewarm. Beat in the egg yolks slowly. Cook until thick, stirring often. Let cool and add the vanilla, coconut, and nuts. Spread between the layers of a German chocolate cake.

Banana Layer Cake

1 ½ cups mashed ripe banana
½ cup buttermilk or sour cream
2 ½ cups all-purpose flour
3 teaspoons baking powder
1 teaspoon baking soda
1 teaspoon cinnamon

1 teaspoon salt
2 sticks butter or margarine
1 ½ cups sugar
2 eggs
1 cup walnuts, chopped

Preheat oven to 350°. In a bowl, mix the bananas and buttermilk together and set aside. In another bowl, sift together the flour, baking powder, baking soda, cinnamon, and salt; set aside. Beat the butter, sugar, and eggs with a mixer on medium speed for 4 to 5 minutes. Stir in the dry ingredients and banana mixture by thirds until mixed well. Fold in the walnuts. Pour into 3 9-inch greased and floured cake pans. Bake for 25 minutes. Let cool and remove from the pan. Ice each layer with cream cheese frosting.

Serves 10.

Mountain Dew Cake

This recipe is from the mailbox.

1 box orange cake mix

1 small box instant vanilla
   pudding mix

1 cup vegetable oil

4 eggs

1 cup Mountain Dew

Icing

1 stick butter or margarine

1 ½ cups sugar

3 tablespoons cornstarch

1 ½ cups flake coconut

Preheat oven to 350°. Put all the ingredients in a large mixing bowl. Beat on low until mixed, about 1 minute, then turn the mixer to high and beat for 4 minutes. Pour into 3 greased and floured 9-inch cake pans. Bake for 20 to 25 minutes.

To make the icing, cook all the ingredients over medium heat until thickened. Spread over cool layers.

Serves 8.

Pistachio Pudding Cake

2 tablespoons flour
1 box white cake mix
1 small box instant pistachio
   pudding mix

¾ cup apricot nectar
¾ cup vegetable oil
3 large eggs
½ teaspoon lemon flavoring

Topping

1 tablespoon lemon juice
¼ cup sugar
¼ cup apricot nectar

Preheat oven to 350°. Mix the flour, cake mix, and pudding in a bowl. Add the nectar, oil, eggs, and flavoring and beat 5 minutes on medium. Grease and flour a tube pan. Bake for 45 to 50 minutes.

To make the topping, put all the ingredients in a saucepan and bring to a boil. Reduce the heat and simmer for 4 to 5 minutes. Pour topping over the hot cake in the pan.

Serves 8 to 10.

Fresh Apple Cake

Another recipe from the mailbox.

2 ½ cups all-purpose flour

2 teaspoons baking powder

1 teaspoon baking soda

1 teaspoon salt

1 teaspoon cinnamon

1 teaspoon nutmeg

1 cup oil

2 cups sugar

3 large eggs, slightly beaten

1 teaspoon lemon flavoring

3 cups chopped raw apples

1 cup chopped walnuts

Preheat oven to 350°. Sift together the flour, baking powder, baking soda, salt, cinnamon, and nutmeg. Set aside. Put the oil in a mixing bowl. Add the sugar and eggs. Mix well and stir in the lemon flavoring. Add the dry ingredients. Beat very well. Add the apples and nuts. Stir well. Pour into a well-greased and floured Bundt pan. Bake 50 to 60 minutes.

Serves 10.

Orange Cake

3 cups flour

3 teaspoons baking powder

¼ teaspoon baking soda

¼ teaspoon salt

2 sticks butter, softened

2 cups sugar

4 eggs

1 cup milk

1 teaspoon orange extract

1 teaspoon grated orange peel

Preheat oven to 350°. Sift together the flour, baking powder, baking soda, and salt and set aside. In a mixing bowl, beat the butter and sugar together. Add the eggs one at a time, beating 1 minute after each. Add the flour mixture and milk in thirds then add orange extract and peel. Stir to mix. Grease and flour 3 9-inch cake pans. Bake for 35 minutes. Cool on racks. Frost with orange cream cheese icing (see the following recipe).

Serves 12.

Orange Cream Cheese Icing

All ingredients should be at room temperature.

1 package (8 ounces) cream cheese, softened

1 box powdered sugar

1 teaspoon pure orange extract

orange juice (if needed)

Combine all the ingredients in a mixing bowl and beat until fluffy, thinning with orange juice if needed.

Orange Cake Layers

2 sticks butter
1 ½ cups sugar
4 eggs
4 cups all-purpose flour
2 teaspoons baking powder

½ teaspoon baking soda
½ teaspoon salt
½ cup orange juice
½ cup water

Orange Cake Filling

1 ½ cups sugar
¼ cup flour
3 tablespoons butter, melted
⅔ cup fresh orange juice

2 eggs, beaten
2 teaspoons grated orange rind
¼ cup lemon juice
pinch of salt

Preheat oven to 350°. Cream butter and sugar until fluffy. Beat in eggs one at a time for 1 minute with a wooden spoon. Mix together the flour, baking powder, baking soda, and salt and set aside. Combine the orange juice and water. Stir the flour and orange juice into the batter by thirds, mixing until well blended. Pour the batter into 3 greased and floured 8- or 9-inch pans. Bake for 30 minutes.

To make the filling, stir together the sugar, flour, and butter in a small pot. Add the orange juice and eggs. Beat together well. Cook over medium heat until thick and smooth, stirring and not allowing the mixture to stick. Stir in the orange rind, lemon juice, and salt. Let cool before spreading on cake layers.

Serves 12.

Pineapple Cake

2½ cups all-purpose flour
2½ teaspoons baking powder
1 teaspoon salt
2½ cups sugar

2 sticks butter, softened
4 eggs
¾ cup milk
1 teaspoon lemon flavoring

Pineapple Filling

½ stick butter
2 tablespoons cornstarch
pinch salt
1 can (15¼ ounces) crushed pineapple

Powdered Sugar Icing

½ stick butter
1 teaspoon vanilla extract
1 box (1 pound) 10x powdered sugar
2–3 tablespoons hot milk

Preheat oven to 350°. Sift together the flour, baking powder, and salt and set aside. With a mixer, cream the sugar and butter until light and fluffy. Add the eggs one at a time and beat after each addition. Stir in a third of the flour mixture then a third of the milk and repeat until all the flour and milk is incorporated. Add the lemon flavoring. Pour an equal amount of batter into each of 3 greased and floured cake pans. Bake for 20 to 25 minutes.

To make the filling, cook all the ingredients in a saucepan over medium heat. Reduce the heat and simmer until thickened. Set aside.

For the icing, cream together all of the ingredients and spread over the cake layers. Spread the pineapple filling between each iced layer and the remainder on top of the cake.

Serves 10.

Apricot Upside-Down Cake

½ stick butter
1 cup brown sugar
1 tablespoon cornstarch
1 quart apricots, drained and
    with the juice reserved

1 box yellow cake mix, prepared
    as directed but using apricot
    juice in place of water

Melt the butter in a large, round cast-iron frying pan. Add the brown sugar, cornstarch, and apricots. Spread evenly in the pan and pour the cake batter over evenly. Bake according to the directions on the cake mix box. Let cool for a bit. Then turn onto a large cake dish.

Serves 8 to 10.

Peach Upside-Down Cake

3 eggs
1½ tablespoons self-rising flour
1 box yellow cake mix
1½ cups water

½ stick butter
1½ cups brown sugar
2 cans peaches (15½ ounces each),
    drained

Preheat oven to 375°. In a mixing bowl, beat the eggs one at a time. Add the flour, cake mix, and water and beat until well mixed. Melt the butter in a 10-inch skillet and stir in the brown sugar. Layer the peaches in the pan and pour the cake mixture over it. Bake for 30 to 40 minutes until brown.

Serves 8.

Pineapple-Carrot-Raisin Layer Cake

2 cups sugar

1¼ cups vegetable oil

2 eggs

2 cups all-purpose flour

2 teaspoons baking powder

½ teaspoon baking soda

2 teaspoons cinnamon

2 cups grated carrot

1 cup raisins

1 cup crushed pineapple,
  drained well

Filling

1 stick butter, softened

1 package (8 ounces) cream
  cheese, softened

1 box (1 pound) powdered sugar

2 tablespoons crushed pineapple

pinch salt

1 cup chopped walnuts

Preheat oven to 350°. In a bowl, mix together the sugar, oil, and eggs. In another bowl, mix together the dry ingredients and gradually add to the sugar mixture. Fold in the carrots, raisins, and pineapple. Pour into 3 9-inch greased and floured pans. Bake for 25 minutes.

To make the filling, cream together the butter, cream cheese, powdered sugar, pineapple, and salt. Spread between the cake layers and on top. Sprinkle the top with walnuts.

Serves 10 to 12.

Poppy Seed Cake

1 small box instant vanilla
pudding mix
1 box yellow cake mix
2 tablespoons flour
1 cup walnuts, crushed

2 eggs, beaten
½ cup vegetable oil
1 cup sour cream
⅓ cup poppy seeds
1 tablespoon vanilla extract

Topping

1 cup powdered sugar
pinch salt
½ teaspoon vanilla extract
2 tablespoons warm water

Preheat oven to 350°. In a bowl, mix together the pudding mix, cake mix, and flour on low. Add all the other ingredients and beat on medium high for five minutes. Pour into a greased and floured tube pan and bake for 1 hour until done.

Mix together the topping ingredients and pour over the cake while hot.

Serves 10.

Pumpkin Tube Cake

3 cups sugar
1 cup vegetable oil
4 eggs
1 can (15¾ ounces) pumpkin
3¼ cups self-rising flour

1 teaspoon baking soda
3 tablespoons cinnamon
½ teaspoon ground cloves
⅔ cup buttermilk
1 cup chopped pecans

Preheat oven to 350°. Mix together the sugar and oil. Add the remaining ingredients and mix until well blended. Pour into a well-greased tube pan and bake for 1 hour or until done.

Serves 8.

Pumpkin Layer Cake

2½ cups all-purpose flour
1 teaspoon baking soda
1 teaspoon baking powder
½ teaspoon salt
1 teaspoon ground cloves

1 teaspoon cinnamon
2 cups sugar
6 eggs, beaten
2½ cups mashed pumpkin
1 cup chopped walnuts

Preheat oven to 350°. Sift together the flour, baking soda, baking powder, salt, cloves, and cinnamon. Put the sugar and eggs in another bowl and beat until fluffy. Add the pumpkin and stir to mix. Mix in the flour mixture. Dust the walnuts with a little flour and stir in. Pour into 3 8-inch greased and floured cake pans. Bake for 15 minutes. Cool and ice with chocolate frosting.

Serves 8.

Banana-Pineapple-Nut Cake

3 cups all-purpose flour
1 teaspoon baking soda
1 teaspoon salt
2¼ cups sugar
1½ teaspoons cinnamon
2 eggs, beaten

1½ cups vegetable oil
1 cup crushed pineapple, drained,
   with juice reserved for topping
1 cup chopped pecans
1 teaspoon vanilla extract
2 cups mashed bananas

Topping

2 tablespoons butter or margarine
2½ tablespoons powdered sugar
½ cup brown sugar
juice from pineapples

Preheat oven to 350°. Mix the dry ingredients together in a large bowl. Make a well in the center of the dry ingredients. Put in the eggs, oil, pineapple, pecans, vanilla, and bananas and stir to mix. Do not beat. Stir until well blended. Grease and flour a tube pan and bake for 1 hour and 15 minutes.

To make the topping, add the ingredients to a saucepan over medium heat. Stir and let come to a boil, then reduce heat to low. Let cook for 4 to 5 minutes. Add more water or sugar if needed. Spread over the cake while warm.

Serves 8 to 10.

Brown Sugar Pound Cake

2 sticks butter, softened
½ cup Crisco shortening
1 box (10 ounces) light brown
　sugar
5 eggs
3½ cups all-purpose flour
1 heaping teaspoon baking
　powder

½ teaspoon salt
¼ teaspoon ginger
1½ cups walnuts, chopped fine
1 teaspoon vanilla extract
1 teaspoon lemon flavoring

Preheat oven to 325°. Beat the butter and shortening together on medium. Add the brown sugar, making sure it's free of lumps. Mix until fluffy, about 10 to 12 minutes. Add the eggs one at a time and mix well to blend after each addition. Sift together the flour, baking powder, salt, ginger, and nuts onto wax paper. Add the vanilla and lemon to the butter mixture. Turn the mixer to low and add the flour 1 cup at a time, mixing after each addition. Pour into greased and floured tube pan and bake for 1 hour and 25 minutes.

Serves 10 to 12.

Prune Pound Cake

2¼ cups all-purpose flour
1 teaspoon baking soda
1 teaspoon allspice
1½ cups sugar
1 cup vegetable oil

3 large eggs
1 cup buttermilk
1 cup prunes, cooked and
    chopped, cooled
1 teaspoon vanilla extract

Preheat oven to 350°. Sift together the flour, baking soda, and allspice into a bowl to blend well. In another bowl, beat the sugar, oil, and eggs 5 minutes on high speed. Reduce the speed to medium and add the flour and buttermilk in thirds. Stir in the prunes and vanilla. Pour into a greased and floured tube pan and bake for 50 minutes or until the cake tests done.

Serves 10.

Sour Cream Pound Cake

2 sticks butter, softened
2¾ cups sugar
5 eggs
½ teaspoon lemon extract
3 cups all-purpose flour

¼ teaspoon baking soda
½ teaspoon salt
1 cup sour cream, divided
½ teaspoon vanilla extract

Preheat oven to 325°. In a mixing bowl, beat the butter on medium until fluffy. Add the sugar one cup at a time, beating well after each addition, until fluffy. Scrape down the sides of the bowl. Add one egg at a time, beating until each is well blended. Add the lemon extract. Mix the flour, baking soda, and salt in a bowl. Turn the mixer to low. Add the flour mixture one cup at a time along with half the sour cream. Mix the last cup of flour with the remaining sour cream and add. Scrape down sides of bowl to blend in flour, and stir in the vanilla. Pour into a greased and floured 10-inch tube pan and bake for 1 hour and 10 minutes. Drizzle with white chocolate icing (page 222).

Serves 8 to 10.

Old-Fashioned Lemon Pound Cake

3 cups sugar
1 pound butter
11 eggs

3½ cups all-purpose flour
2 teaspoons lemon extract
1 tablespoon lemon juice

Preheat oven to 325°. Cream the sugar and butter. Add the eggs one at a time, beating after each addition. Add the flour a little at a time. Beat until well blended. Add the lemon extract and lemon juice. Pour into a well-greased and floured tube pan. Bake for one hour and 20 minutes.

Serves 8 to 10.

Quick Lemon Pound Cake

1 yellow cake mix
1 small box instant lemon
   pudding mix

4 large eggs
½ cup vegetable oil
1 teaspoon lemon flavoring

Topping

juice of 1 lemon
juice of 1 orange
½ cup sugar

Preheat oven to 350°. Blend all of the ingredients on medium speed. Pour into a tube pan and bake for 45 minutes.

To make the topping, mix together the lemon juice and orange juice. Add the sugar and stir to mix well. Pour over the cake immediately after removing it from the oven. Let the cake cool before removing from the pan.

Serves 8 to 10.

Pineapple Filling

1 tablespoon butter or margarine
2 tablespoons cornstarch
½ cup sugar

2 cups crushed pineapple
   with juice
few drops lemon juice

Cook all the ingredients together in a saucepan over medium heat. Reduce the heat to simmer for 10 minutes until the juice is clear. Cool slightly and spread between cake layers. Spread the sides and top of the cake with buttercream icing.

Lemon Filling

1 cup sugar
5 tablespoons flour
1 large egg, beaten
⅓ cup lemon juice

½ stick butter
⅔ cup water
¼ cup Cool Whip

In the top of a double broiler over medium heat, combine the sugar and flour. Stir in the egg, lemon juice, butter, and water. Stir to mix. Cook 10 to 12 minutes over boiling water, then remove from the heat and chill. Fold in the Cool Whip and spread on the cake.

Lemon Curd

This is for a lemon cake.

1 cup sugar
1 cup fresh lemon juice
   (from 5–6 lemons)

1 tablespoon grated lemon rind
½ stick butter, melted
3 eggs, beaten

Combine the sugar, lemon juice, and lemon rind in a saucepan. Stir in the butter and eggs and cook over medium heat, stirring constantly until thickened. The curd is ready when it coats the spoon. Do not boil. Pour into a container while hot. Cover and refrigerate.

Chocolate Fudge Icing I

3 blocks semisweet chocolate,
   melted
2 sticks butter, softened
1 box (1 pound) powdered sugar,
   sifted

½ cup hot milk
1 teaspoon vanilla extract
pinch salt

Melt the chocolate in a double boiler over hot water. Stir in the
butter then add the sugar and as much hot milk as needed for desired
consistency. Beat until shiny. Stir in the vanilla and salt. Spread
between layers and around the sides of the cake.

Chocolate Fudge Icing II

2 cups sugar
⅓ cup cocoa
½ cup milk

1 stick butter, melted
pinch of salt

Combine the sugar and cocoa in a saucepan. Stir in the milk, butter,
and salt. Cook the mixture over medium heat, stirring all the while.
Let boil hard for 1 minute. Beat with a mixer until spreadable.

Cocoa Chocolate Icing

3 cups sugar
⅔ cup cocoa
1 cup evaporated milk
1 ½ sticks butter, melted

Mix the sugar and cocoa together in a pot. Stir in the evaporated milk and butter and heat over medium high heat just until the boiling point. Stir the mixture for 3 minutes, then pour it into a small bowl set in cold water. When cool, beat with a mixer until thick enough to spread. Add a little water if needed.

Cooked Chocolate Icing

2 cups sugar
¾ cup evaporated milk
2 squares unsweetened chocolate
2 tablespoons light corn syrup

1 teaspoon vanilla extract
2 tablespoons butter
pinch salt

Combine all of the ingredients in a saucepan. Cook over medium heat for 12 to 15 minutes, stirring constantly. Beat until shiny. Spread over cake.

White Chocolate Icing

1 package (4 ounces) white chocolate, chopped
2 tablespoons butter

Melt the chocolate and butter in the top of a double boiler. Remove from the heat and drizzle over cooled cake.

Fluffy White Icing

4 tablespoons flour
1 cup milk
½ cup shortening
1 stick butter

1 cup sugar
½ teaspoon salt
2 teaspoons vanilla extract

Blend the flour into the milk and set aside. Cream the shortening, butter, and sugar well, and add the salt and vanilla. Cook over medium heat until the mixture reaches the consistency of cream. Cool and add the flour mixture, beating until very fluffy.

Caramel Icing

This old-fashioned icing is still a treat.

3 cups brown sugar
2 sticks butter
1½ cups evaporated milk
pinch salt

Put all of the ingredients in a large saucepan over medium heat and stir until the sugar melts. Cook slowly for 10 to 12 minutes. The icing is done when a small amount dropped into cold water forms a ball. Remove the icing from the heat and beat with a mixer on medium until thick and creamy. Spread between the layers and on the top and sides of the cake.

Orange Icing

2 tablespoons butter
1½ cups sugar
5 tablespoons flour
pinch salt

⅔ cup fresh orange juice
2 eggs, beaten
¼ cup lemon juice
2 teaspoons grated orange rind

In a saucepan, stir together the butter, sugar, flour, and salt. Add the orange juice and eggs and beat together well. Cook over medium heat, stirring often, until thick and smooth. Remove from the heat and stir in the lemon juice and orange rind. Let cool and spread over cake layers.

Buttercream Frosting

2 cups powdered sugar
½ teaspoon vanilla extract
2 tablespoons milk

1 stick butter, melted
pinch salt

In a bowl, combine all of the ingredients until well blended. Add more milk if needed. Spread over the cake.

Cooked Butter Icing

3 cups sugar
pinch salt
¾ cup evaporated milk

2 sticks butter
1 teaspoon vanilla extract

Put the sugar, salt, and milk in a saucepan over medium high heat. Cut in the butter, stir until melted, and bring to a boil. Let the mixture boil hard for 4 minutes, stirring the entire time. Remove from the heat and set the pan in cold water. Stir in the vanilla. Beat with a mixer until the icing is thick enough to spread. If it gets too hard, stir in a few drops of water. If it is too soft, stir in a small amount of sifted powdered sugar.

Chocolate Pie

1¾ cups sugar
½ cup cocoa
1 cup evaporated milk
1 stick butter

3 eggs, lightly beaten
pinch salt
1 teaspoon vanilla extract
1 unbaked 9-inch pie shell

Preheat oven to 350°. Mix together the sugar and cocoa. Stir in the milk, butter, eggs, salt, and vanilla and blend well. Pour into the crust and bake for 45 minutes. Serve warm or cold with whipped topping.

Serves 8.

Mince Meat Pie

This is a Thanksgiving treat that is gone but not forgotten. Mincemeat was often made in the kitchen and canned in jars, along with other fruits and vegetables.

2 unbaked 9-inch piecrusts
1 jar (32 ounces) mincemeat
2 cups chopped firm apples

2 tablespoons butter, melted
½ cup brown sugar
1 teaspoon lemon juice

Preheat the oven to 375°. Bake the bottom crust for 8 minutes. Mix the mincemeat, apples, butter, brown sugar, and lemon juice and put into the crust. Lay the top crust over the filling and make a few slits in it. Bake about 40 to 50 minutes. Serve with whipped topping or cheddar cheese.

Serves 8.

Chess Pie

½ cup sugar
1 cup light brown sugar
2 tablespoons cornstarch
1 stick butter, melted
4 eggs, beaten

¼ cup milk
1 teaspoon vanilla extract
1 unbaked 9-inch deep-dish
   pie shell

Preheat oven to 325°. Mix the sugar, brown sugar, and cornstarch together. Stir in the butter and eggs and mix well. Stir in the milk and vanilla. Pour into the pie shell and bake for 40 minutes.

Serves 6 to 8.

Lemon Chess Pie

2 sticks butter, softened
1½ cups sugar
1 tablespoon cornmeal
5 eggs, well beaten

¼ cup fresh lemon juice
1 teaspoon grated lemon rind
1 unbaked 9-inch pie shell

Preheat oven to 350°. Cream the butter and sugar together. Add the cornmeal and eggs. Stir in the lemon juice and grated lemon rind and mix well. Pour into the pie shell and bake for 40 minutes or until well browned.

Serves 8.

Chocolate Pie with Cookie Crust

1 package (10 ounces)
   semisweet chocolate
½ cup sugar
¼ cup flour
pinch salt

4 egg yolks, beaten
1½ cups milk
2 tablespoons butter
1 teaspoon vanilla extract
1 chocolate cookie crust

Meringue

4 egg whites, at room temperature
2¼ tablespoons sugar

Preheat oven to 400°. Melt the chocolate in the microwave. Mix the sugar, flour, and salt. Add the egg yolks and milk and cook over low heat, stirring often. When the mixture is hot, stir in the melted chocolate and cook until thickened. Add the butter and vanilla. Stir to blend well. Pour into the cookie crust and top with meringue.

To make the meringue, beat the egg whites until they begin to stiffen and stand in peaks. Do not over beat. Add the sugar gradually. Spread the meringue over the chocolate filling and bake until brown, 10 to 12 minutes.

Serves 8.

Coconut Cream Pie

This is an old-fashioned pie that we still remember fondly.

5 tablespoons flour
1 cup sugar
pinch salt
2 cups milk
3 egg yolks

3 tablespoons butter
1 teaspoon vanilla extract
1 package (6 ounces) shredded
   coconut
1 unbaked 9-inch pie shell

Meringue

4 egg whites, at room temperature
2 ¼ tablespoons sugar

Prick the bottom of the pie shell and bake at 400° for 10 to 12 minutes until brown. Put the flour, sugar, and salt in the top of a double broiler and slowly whisk in the milk, cooking over boiling water and stirring often. Beat the egg yolks in a bowl and add slowly to the mixture, 2 to 3 tablespoons at a time. Remove from the heat and stir in the butter, vanilla, and coconut. Pour into the pie shell.

To make the meringue topping, beat the egg whites until they begin to stiffen and stand in peaks. Do not over beat. Add the sugar gradually, then spread over the pie, gently pressing the meringue over the edges. Bake at 300° for 15 to 20 minutes until brown.

Serves 8.

Coconut-Pineapple Pie

3 eggs
3 tablespoons flour
1 cup sugar
2 tablespoons butter, melted
1 cup crushed pineapple, drained

1 cup coconut
1 cup milk
pinch salt
1 unbaked 9-inch pie shell

Preheat oven to 350°. In a bowl, beat the eggs well. Mix the flour and sugar together and blend into the eggs. Stir in all other ingredients and mix well. Pour into the pie shell and bake for 35 to 40 minutes until brown.

Serves 8.

Chocolate Pecan Pie

2 squares unsweetened chocolate
1 stick butter
¾ cup sugar
1 cup light corn syrup
4 large eggs, beaten

1 teaspoon vanilla extract
1 cup coarsely chopped
   pecan meats
1 unbaked 9-inch pie shell

Preheat oven to 350°. Melt the chocolate with the butter in the top of a double boiler. Remove from the heat and stir in the sugar and corn syrup. Mix well. Add the eggs and mix well. Stir in the vanilla and nuts and pour into the pie shell. Bake for 35 minutes. Serve with whipped topping or vanilla ice cream.

Serves 8.

Sweet Potato-Pecan-Coconut Pie

1 can (15 ounces) mashed yams
¾ cup brown sugar
½ stick butter, melted
1 teaspoon nutmeg
½ teaspoon cinnamon
3 eggs, beaten
¼ cup light corn syrup

1 can (14 ounces) sweetened
    condensed milk
½ cup chopped pecans
½ cup frozen coconut
1 unbaked 9-inch deep-dish
    pie shell

Preheat oven to 350°. In a mixing bowl, combine the yams, brown sugar, butter, nutmeg, and cinnamon and mix well. Add the eggs, corn syrup, and condensed milk and mix well. Stir in the pecans and coconut. Pour into the pie shell and bake for 45 minutes.

Serves 6 to 8.

Lemon Meringue Pie

If you don't have a double boiler you can make one with two different sized pots.

1 ¼ cups sugar
5 tablespoons cornstarch
1 cup milk
4 egg yolks

1 stick butter
6 tablespoons lemon juice
1 unbaked 9-inch pie shell

Meringue

4 egg whites
4 tablespoons sugar
½ teaspoon cream of tartar

Bake the pie shell at 400° for 10 to 12 minutes until brown. In the top of a double boiler mix the sugar and cornstarch. Combine the milk and egg yolks. Stir into the sugar mixture and mix well using a wire whisk. Place over hot water and stir until thickened. Stir in the butter and lemon juice and mix well. Pour into the pie shell.

To make the meringue, beat the egg whites until stiffened, adding the sugar one tablespoon at a time. Add the cream of tartar and beat until the egg whites hold a peak. Pour onto the pie filling and spread evenly.

Serves 8.

Old-Fashioned Apple Pie

In the country, apple pie was often served warm with cheese.

5 cups thinly sliced apple
¾ cup sugar
2 tablespoons flour
¼ tablespoon salt
½ teaspoon nutmeg
¼ cup water

1 teaspoon vanilla extract
1 unbaked 9-inch deep-dish
  pie shell
½ stick cold butter, cut into pieces
1 unbaked piecrust (for top of pie)

Preheat oven to 350°. Mix together the first 7 ingredients and pour into the pie shell. Drop the butter over the apple filling. Add the top crust and cut a few slits in it. Place the pie on aluminum foil or a baking pan and bake for 50 minutes; increase the heat to 375° and bake until brown.

Serves 8.

Apple Pie Crumble

5 cups sliced apple
½ cup water
1 cup sugar
pinch salt

2 tablespoons butter
1 teaspoon nutmeg
1 unbaked 9-inch pie shell

Cheese Crumble Topping

¾ cup all-purpose flour
1 cup grated cheddar cheese
½ stick cold butter

Preheat oven to 350°. Add the apples, water, sugar, and salt to a pot over medium high heat. Cook until just tender. Stir in the butter and nutmeg. Cool and spread into the pie shell.

Mix all of the topping ingredients together and spread over the apple filling. Bake for 45 to 50 minutes.

Serves 8.

French Apple Pie

5 cups thinly sliced apples
¼ cup + 1 tablespoon water
¾ cup sugar
1 cup raisins
1 tablespoon flour
½ teaspoon lemon flavoring

½ teaspoon cinnamon
½ stick butter
1 unbaked 9-inch pie shell
   with top crust
1 cup powdered sugar

Preheat oven to 375°. Put the apples, ¼ cup water, and sugar in a pot over medium heat. Cover and cook until very hot, then remove from heat. Mix together the raisins, flour, lemon flavoring, cinnamon, and butter in a bowl while the apples cool a bit. Pour the apples into the pie shell, then pour the raisin mixture over the apple filling. Lay the top crust over the filling and make a few slits in it. Place the pie on aluminum foil or a baking pan then bake for 45 minutes until brown. Mix the powdered sugar with 1 tablespoon water and spread over the pie.

Serves 8.

Easy Boston Cream Pie

This will make 2 8-inch cakes.

1 box white cake mix
1 tablespoon flour

1 large box vanilla pudding (not instant), prepared as directed

Chocolate Icing

2 cups powdered sugar
3 teaspoons cocoa
2 tablespoons milk

3 tablespoons butter, melted
pinch salt

Preheat oven to 350°. Mix the cake mix with the flour and prepare the batter as directed on the package. Pour into 2 8-inch round cake pans or iron skillets and bake as directed. Test for doneness. Let the cakes cool completely, then split them in half and fill with the pudding.

Stir together all of the icing ingredients and spread over the top of each cake.

Serves 8.

Fresh Peach Pie

3 tablespoons flour
¾ cup sugar
pinch salt
5 cups fresh peaches, sliced

¼ teaspoon almond extract
2 unbaked 9-inch piecrusts
¾ stick cold butter, cut into
  pieces

Preheat oven to 375°. Mix the flour, sugar, and salt together in a bowl and add the peaches and almond extract, stirring to mix well. Pour into the pie shell. Drop the butter over the peach filling and add the top crust, making a few slits in it. Place the pie on a baking pan or aluminum foil and bake for 45 minutes until brown.

Serves 8.

Sweet Potato—Pumpkin Pie

1 can (15¾ ounces) pumpkin
1 cup mashed yams
½ stick butter, melted
1 can (14 ounces) sweetened
  condensed milk

¾ cup packed brown sugar
2 teaspoons cinnamon
3 eggs, beaten
2 unbaked 9-inch deep-dish
  pie shells

Preheat oven to 325°. Put the pumpkin, yams, butter, condensed milk, brown sugar, and cinnamon in a bowl. Mix together well and stir in the eggs. Pour into the pie shell and bake for 1 hour.

Serves 8.

Sweet Potato–Coconut Pie

2 cups mashed cooked sweet
  potatoes
½ stick butter, melted
½ cup sugar
¼ cup corn syrup
2 eggs, beaten

1 cup milk
pinch salt
1 teaspoon nutmeg
¼ teaspoon ginger
1 cup frozen coconut
1 unbaked 9-inch pie shell

Preheat oven to 350°. Put the potatoes in a bowl and add the butter, sugar, corn syrup, eggs, milk, salt, nutmeg, and ginger. Mix well. Stir in the coconut and pour into the pie shell. Bake for 40 minutes or until set.

Serves 8.

Sweet Potato Custard Pie

2 cups cooked mashed fresh
  or canned yams
1 can (14 ounces) sweetened
  condensed milk
½ cup sugar
½ stick butter

½ cup milk
1 teaspoon vanilla extract
½ teaspoon nutmeg
¼ teaspoon rum flavoring
4 eggs, beaten
1 unbaked 9-inch pie shell

Preheat oven to 375°. In a bowl, mix all ingredients except the pie shell together. Pour into the pie shell and bake for 40 minutes until brown.

Serves 6 to 8.

White Potato Pie

When the sweet potatoes began to sprout for planting, it was harvest time for many white potatoes. Use baking potatoes for this pie as they mash fluffier.

2½ cups mashed russet potatoes, peeled and cut into quarters
½ stick butter, melted
1½ cups sugar
¼ teaspoon nutmeg
¼ teaspoon cinnamon

1 cup milk
3 eggs, beaten
1 teaspoon lemon flavoring
pinch salt
1 unbaked 8-inch pie shell

Preheat oven to 375°. Put the potatoes in a pot, cover with water, and cook slowly until tender. Drain and peel. Put the potatoes in a bowl, add the butter, and mash while hot. In another bowl, mix the sugar with the nutmeg and cinnamon. Stir in the potatoes. Stir in the milk, eggs, lemon flavoring, and salt. Pour into the pie shell and bake for 40 to 50 minutes or until set and brown.

Serves 8.

Cherry-Rhubarb Cobbler

3 tablespoons cornstarch
2 tablespoons water
2 cans (15 ounces each)
  unsweetened cherries,
  with juice reserved
1½ cups sugar

3 tablespoons butter, melted
pinch salt
½ teaspoon lemon juice
1 stalk rhubarb, sliced into
  ½-inch pieces
1 unbaked 9-inch piecrust

Preheat oven to 375°. Combine the cornstarch and water and set aside. Put the juice from the cherries, sugar, butter, salt, and lemon juice in a saucepan over medium heat and stir to mix. When it comes to a boil, stir in the cornstarch mixture to thicken. Remove from the heat and stir in the cherries and rhubarb. Pour into a 9 × 13 × 2-inch baking dish. Roll out the crust cut into 1-inch strips. Make a lattice top by laying the strips across the top of the dish; cut off the excess. Flip the ends and pull up the bottom to seal. Bake on aluminum foil or a baking pan on a low rack in the oven for about 40 minutes.

Serves 8.

Tomato Cobbler

This is another old-fashioned dish that we have not forgotten.

5 cups firm ripe tomatoes
½ cup sugar
1 cup light brown sugar
2 tablespoons flour
¼ teaspoon salt

½ teaspoon ground ginger
½ teaspoon nutmeg
2 unbaked 9-inch deep-dish
  piecrusts
½ stick cold butter, cut into pieces

Preheat oven to 375°. Dip the tomatoes in very hot water then cool and peel. Squeeze the seeds from the tomatoes and dice the flesh. Mix the sugar, brown sugar, flour, salt, ginger, and nutmeg. Put the tomatoes in one of the piecrusts and pour the sugar mixture over the top. Dot with the butter and lay the top crust over the filling. Bake until brown, about 50 minutes.

Serves 8.

Piecrust

3 cups all-purpose flour
1 cup shortening
1 teaspoon salt

2 teaspoons sugar
¼ cup cold water

In a bowl, mix the flour and shortening with a fork or your fingertips to form large pieces. Stir in the salt, sugar, and water and mix just enough to form a ball. Freezes well.

Fresh Blackberry Dessert

4 cups blackberries
1 cup self-rising flour
¾ cup sugar

pinch salt
½ stick butter, melted

Preheat oven to 375°. Spread the berries in a 9 × 13-inch baking pan. Mix the flour, sugar, and salt in a bowl. Add the butter and work in with fingertips until crumbly. Spread evenly over the berries. Bake for 40 minutes until brown.

Serves 8.

Deep-Dish Apricot Dessert

2 cans (10½ ounce each) apricot
  in syrup
3 ounces cream cheese
1½ teaspoons cinnamon

1 box yellow cake mix
1 cup brown sugar
¾ stick butter, melted

Preheat oven to 350°. Pour the apricots with their syrup into a 9 × 13-inch baking dish. In a bowl, mix together the cream cheese, cinnamon, and cake mix until coarse and crumbly. Sprinkle evenly over the apricots. Sprinkle with the brown sugar and drizzle the butter over the apricots. Bake for 45 to 50 minutes. Serve warm with ice cream.

Serves 8 to 10.

Apple Brown Betty

1 stick butter, melted
1 cup sugar
1 ½ cups brown sugar
1 teaspoon cinnamon
4 eggs, beaten

2 cups milk
4 cups sliced apples
2 teaspoons vanilla extract
1 cup raisins
4 cups bread cut into cubes

Preheat oven to 350°. Put the butter in a bowl and add the sugar, brown sugar, cinnamon, and eggs. Mix well. Stir in the milk and apples; stir in the vanilla, raisins, and bread. Let set for 15 minutes then pour into a 9 × 13-inch baking pan and bake for 40 minutes.

Serves 8.

Apple Bread Pudding

4 cups hard bread cut into cubes
2 pounds mixed apples,
    peeled and cut into 8 pieces
1 cup raisins
1 ½ cups light brown sugar
2 teaspoons cinnamon

1 teaspoon nutmeg
1 stick butter, melted
4 eggs, beaten
2 cups milk
1 teaspoon lemon flavoring

Layer half of the bread in the bottom of a 9 × 13 × 2-inch baking pan. In a bowl, mix together the apples, raisins, sugar, cinnamon, and nutmeg until well coated. Spread over the bread. Top with the remaining bread cubes. Mix together the butter, eggs, milk, and lemon flavoring and pour over the bread. Cover and let set 2 hours or overnight in the refrigerator. Bake covered at 375° for 40 minutes. Serve warm.

Serves 10.

Coconut Bread Pudding

8 slices white bread, diced
1 can (14 ounces) sweetened
 condensed milk, heated
½ stick butter, melted
2 cups sugar

4 eggs, beaten well
3 cups milk
½ teaspoon nutmeg
1 teaspoon vanilla extract
2 cups frozen coconut

Preheat oven to 350°. Put the bread in a bowl and pour in the heated condensed milk. Add the butter and stir lightly; let cool. Combine the sugar, eggs, milk, nutmeg, and vanilla in a bowl. Stir to mix well and add the coconut. Bake for 40 to 45 minutes.

Serves 8.

Egg Noodle Pudding

This is my version of a dessert kugel that was served at the community dinner.

4 eggs, beaten
1 cup milk
1 stick butter or margarine, melted
2 cups light brown sugar
1 teaspoon cinnamon
1 package (16 ounces) broad egg noodles, prepared as directed
1 cup raisins, soaked for 10 minutes in hot water and drained
1 apple, grated or chopped fine

Preheat oven to 350°. Combine the eggs and milk. Add the butter, sugar, and cinnamon and mix well. Stir in the remaining ingredients and pour into a buttered baking dish for 30 minutes. Cut into squares to serve.

Serves 8.

Chocolate Bread Pudding

4 cups crumbled day-old bread

3 cups milk

1 small can (5 ounces) evaporated milk

2 cups sugar

6 tablespoons cocoa

1 stick butter, melted

½ cup chocolate syrup

3 eggs, beaten

1 teaspoon vanilla extract

½ cup chopped macadamia nuts (optional)

Put the bread in a bowl with the milk and evaporated milk and set aside for 30 minutes. Preheat the oven to 350°. Mix the sugar and cocoa, then stir in the remaining ingredients. Pour into a baking dish and bake for 40 minutes. Serve warm.

Serves 8.

Dessert Waffles with Ice Cream and Chocolate

1½ cups all-purpose flour

2 teaspoons baking powder

1 teaspoon salt

1 stick butter or margarine

½ cup sugar

2 eggs, beaten

1 cup milk

2 ounces chocolate squares, melted

Preheat the waffle iron. Sift the flour, baking powder, and salt into a bowl and set aside. In another bowl, cream the butter and sugar. Add the eggs and mix well. Stir in the milk. Stir in the flour mixture and melted chocolate until well mixed. Pour into the hot waffle iron and cook 3 to 4 minutes. Serve with vanilla ice cream, chocolate syrup, and chopped pecans.

Serves 4.

Butterscotch Cookies

These cookies were in most homes with kids—ready to bake.

1 stick butter
¼ cup shortening
⅔ cup sugar
½ pound brown sugar
1 pound all-purpose flour

1 teaspoon cream of tarter
1 teaspoon baking soda
2 eggs
1 teaspoon vanilla extract
¼ cup pecans, chopped fine

Cream the butter and shortening on medium speed until just mixed, about 5 minutes. Mix the dry ingredients together. Add the eggs and vanilla to the butter mixture and mix well. Add the dry ingredients and mix on low until well blended. Fold in the pecans. Form the dough into two long rolls 2 inches in diameter and wrap in plastic wrap or wax paper. Refrigerate overnight. Slice the dough with a sharp knife into ½-inch pieces and bake on a cookie sheet at 375° for 8 to 10 minutes.

Makes 4 dozen 2-inch cookies.

Apple-Nut Squares

3 eggs
¾ cup brown sugar
1 tablespoon vanilla extract
½ teaspoon salt

1½ cups self-rising flour
4 cups chopped apples
1½ cups walnuts

Preheat oven to 350°. Break the eggs into a bowl and beat until foamy. Add the brown sugar, vanilla, and salt and mix well. Stir in the flour. Add the apples and walnuts. Pour into a greased and floured 9 × 13-inch baking pan. Bake for 25 minutes until brown.

Makes 12 squares.

Coconut Squares

3¼ cups graham cracker crumbs
¾ cup unsalted butter, melted
3 cups flake coconut
1½ cups sweetened condensed milk

¼ cup semisweet chocolate chips,
   melted with ½ teaspoon butter
5 tablespoons powdered sugar

Preheat oven to 350°. Put the graham crackers and butter in a bowl and mix well. Grease a 12 × 18-inch baking pan. Pour in the graham cracker mixture and press down evenly. Sprinkle the coconut over the crust. Punch holes in the crust with a fork and slowly pour the condensed milk evenly over the coconut. Bake for 20 minutes, but do not brown. Mix the chocolate chips with the powdered sugar. Drizzle the chocolate mixture over the coconut. Cool and cut into squares.

Makes 36 squares.

Brownies with Macadamia Nuts

2 sticks butter or margarine
4 ounces semisweet chocolate
2 cups sugar
4 eggs, beaten

1 cup self-rising flour
16 ounces macadamia nuts
2 teaspoons vanilla extract

Preheat oven to 325°. Melt the butter and chocolate together over low heat and add the other ingredients. Mix well and pour into a greased and floured baking pan and bake for 30 minutes.

Makes 12 brownies.

Baked Fudge

This is good served with ice cream.

1 stick butter
2 squares unsweetened chocolate
2 eggs, beaten
1 cup sugar

¼ cup flour
pinch salt
1 teaspoon vanilla extract

Preheat oven to 350°. Melt the butter and chocolate over low heat. Put the eggs in a bowl and add the sugar, flour, salt, and vanilla. Stir in the chocolate mixture and pour into a greased pie plate. Bake for 20 minutes.

Serves 8.

Heavenly Hash

1 jar (4 ounces) maraschino
  cherries
3 ripe firm bananas
1 tablespoon lemon juice
1 large container (12 ounces)
  Cool Whip

1 package (16 ounces) mini
  marshmallows
1 large can (12 ounces) crushed
  pineapple
1 cup pecan pieces

Dice the cherries and bananas, put them in a bowl, and pour the lemon juice over the fruit. Mix in the remaining ingredients and chill.

Serves 8 to 10.

Ice Box Dessert

4½ cups milk
2 small boxes instant vanilla
  pudding mix

1 container (8 ounces) sour cream
1 box chocolate graham crackers

Topping

½ cup cocoa
5 tablespoons milk
1 cup sugar

1 teaspoon vanilla extract
½ stick butter

Heat the milk and add the pudding mix. Stir until lightly thickened. Add the sour cream to the pudding and mix well, stirring from the bottom. Spread a layer of graham crackers in the bottom of a 2-quart casserole dish, and then add a layer of pudding over the graham crackers. Continue adding layers of crackers and pudding, ending with a layer of pudding.

To make the topping, heat all the ingredients in a saucepan over low heat. Bring to a boil and cook for about 1 minute, then remove from heat and spread over the graham crackers and pudding.

Serves 8.

Banana Split Dessert

3 small boxes instant French
  vanilla pudding mix
4 cups milk
1 container (8 ounces) sour cream
½ container (about 4 ounces) of
  Cool Whip

1 box chocolate wafers
4 bananas, ripe but firm
1 package (10 ounces) frozen
  sliced strawberries
1 package frozen coconut
powered sugar for sprinkling

Combine the pudding and the milk and mix well. Stir in the sour
cream and fold in the Cool Whip. Layer the chocolate wafers on the
bottom and sides of a 9 × 13-inch pan or dish. Slice and layer in the
bananas. Spread a third of the pudding mixture over the bananas and
then begin adding layers of the strawberries, wafers, bananas, coconut,
and pudding until all the ingredients are used. Top with coconut
and sprinkle with powdered sugar. This tastes best when allowed to
mellow overnight in the refrigerator.

Serves 6 to 8.

Peach Dessert

1 large angel food cake
1 stick butter, softened
1 cup powdered sugar
3 tablespoons milk
¼ cup brown sugar
1 teaspoon almond extract

6 fresh peaches, peeled, sliced
    and mixed with 2 tablespoons
    lemon juice
1 large container whipped
    topping, thawed

Split the cake into 3 layers. Mix together the butter, powdered sugar, milk, brown sugar, and almond extract. Spread half of the mixture on the first cake layer. Top with sliced peaches and whipped topping. Repeat with the other 2 layers, then cover cake all over with whipped topping. Top with more sliced peaches. Refrigerate.

Serves 8.

Vanilla Milkshake

This has become a favorite summertime dessert at Mama Dip's Kitchen.

3 scoops vanilla ice cream
2 teaspoons Splenda
1 teaspoon vanilla extract
¼ cup milk

Mix all the ingredients together in a blender until smooth. You may use a hand mixer instead. Serve immediately in tall glasses.

Makes 14 ounces.

Chocolate-Dipped Fruit

large strawberries
fresh pineapple chunks
seedless grapes
cherries with stems
1 pound semisweet chocolate

Wash and dry the fruit. Melt the chocolate in the top of a double boiler. Dip the fruit in the chocolate and place on wax paper to harden.

Friendship Cake

It takes 30 days to make the starter for this cake. Between the first day and the last, we were constantly gossiping about what was happening and not happening with the cake. Often, one of the members of our church would bring her finished 30-day cake to a church gathering. You can make a friend with this recipe.

On the 1st day: Make the starter by adding 2½ cups sugar and 1 16-ounce can sliced peaches with juice to a 1-gallon container. Stir together, cover, and let stand at room temperature. Do not refrigerate. Stir the mixture every day. The fruit may bubble and pop off. This is normal. Keep covered.

On the 10th day: Add 2 cups sugar and 1 16-ounce can pineapple chunks with juice. Continue to stir every day.

On the 20th day: Add 2 cups sugar and 1 30-ounce can fruit cocktail with juice and 1 10-ounce jar maraschino cherries with juice. Continue to stir every day.

On the 30th day: Drain the fruit, reserving the juice. Divide the fruit into three portions (to be used for the cake). Divide the juice into 1½-cup portions. Place the juice in airtight containers and give to friends with a copy of the recipe as soon as possible. The starter should be used within 5 days. It cannot be frozen.

For each cake:
1 yellow cake mix
1 small box instant vanilla pudding mix
⅔ cup vegetable oil
4 eggs
1½ cups starter
1 cup chopped pecans

Mix all the ingredients together by hand. Bake in a greased and floured Bundt or tube pan at 350° for 50 minutes or until done.

Makes 3 cakes.

Community Suppers and Party Food

Oven Chopped Barbecue

Fried Chicken

Community Dinner Kugel

Cranberry Kugel

Potato Salad

Sweet and Sour Slaw

Apple-Raisin Coleslaw

Limas and Tomatoes

Corn Pudding

Tomato Juice Cocktail

Sausage Wheels

Egg Rolls

Sweet and Sour Meatballs

Sweet and Sour Drumettes

Stuffed Mushrooms

Hamburger Pizza

Ham Pizza

Vegetable Pizza

Cucumber-and-Onion-Filled
    Tomatoes

Shrimp and Spinach Dip

Shrimp Ball

Smoked Oyster Log

Clam Spread

Spam Cheese Log

Dipping Sauce

Fun Dip

Family Christmas
    Greeting Tray

Marshmallow Multigrain
    Cheerios Bar

M&M Popcorn Balls

COMMUNITY SUPPERS were an important part of our social life growing up. They are still popular now—although usually referred to as "potlucks" and other names. The recipes that follow are good dishes to take to a community supper.

Oven Chopped Barbecue

6 – 8 pounds pork Boston butt
½ cup brown sugar
2 cups apple cider vinegar
½ cup mustard

1 teaspoon crushed red pepper
¼ cup Heinz 57 sauce
¼ cup hot sauce

Place the meat on a rack in a large pan. Bake in a 300° oven for 4 hours or until so tender that you can pierce the meat to the bone. Remove from the oven and let cool. Trim the fat; pull the meat from the bone and chop. Mix the remaining ingredients together in a bowl and add the meat. Serve on buns.

Makes about 3 pounds.

Fried Chicken

2½ teaspoons salt

2 cups water

1 whole chicken or chicken parts

1½ cups flour

1 teaspoon black pepper

1½ cups shortening

In a bowl, mix 2 teaspoons of the salt with the water. Add the chicken and soak for 15 to 20 minutes. Drain the chicken and pat it dry. Mix together the flour, pepper, and remaining ½ teaspoon salt. Dip the chicken in the flour mixture to coat, shaking off excess flour. Heat the shortening in a skillet over medium heat. The shortening should be at 350° on a thermometer, or you can test it by dipping a corner of the chicken into the shortening; if the chicken begins to fry, the shortening is ready. Brown the chicken on all sides, reducing the heat if needed. It takes about 20 minutes to fry chicken well done.

Serves 4 to 5.

Community Dinner Kugel

Kugel was a big hit at the annual community dinner in Chapel Hill. This recipe is my version for a side dish. I also created a dessert version (see the recipe for egg noodle pudding in the desserts chapter).

3 eggs, beaten
1 container (8 ounces) sour cream
¼ cup brown sugar
1 teaspoon cinnamon
1 large apple, peeled and chopped
1 cup raisins

1 cup milk
1 package (16 ounces) wide egg
  noodles, cooked as directed
½ stick butter or margarine,
  melted

Preheat oven to 350°. Grease a 2 ½-quart baking pan. Combine the first seven ingredients; mix well. Stir in the cooked noodles and pour the mixture into the pan. Spoon the butter over the noodle mixture and bake uncovered for about 30 minutes until brown. Cut into 2-inch squares. Serve as a side dish.

Serves 6 to 8.

Cranberry Kugel

3 eggs, beaten
2 cups packed brown sugar
¼ teaspoon salt
1 stick butter, melted
1 cup sour cream
1 package (16 ounces) wide egg
noodles, cooked as directed

2 cups dried cranberries
½ cup chopped pecans
½ cup orange juice
4–5 saltine crackers

Preheat oven to 375°. In a bowl, mix together the eggs and brown sugar until well blended. Stir in the salt, butter, and sour cream. Add the noodles, cranberries, pecans, and orange juice. Pour the mixture into a baking dish and sprinkle the crackers over it. Bake for 30 minutes. Let cool and cut into squares.

Serves 8.

Potato Salad

3 pounds potatoes
2 tablespoons chopped sweet
  onions (optional)
1 cup mayonnaise
1 teaspoon salt
1 teaspoon sugar
½ cup chopped celery
1 cup sweet salad cubes
4 hard-boiled eggs, chopped

Put the potatoes in a pot with enough water to cover them and cook until tender. Drain the potatoes and cool them with ice-cold water. Peel and cube the cooled potatoes and put them in a bowl. Add the remaining ingredients and mix well. Refrigerate until ready to serve.

Serves 8.

Sweet and Sour Slaw

8 cups (2 quarts) moderately
  finely grated cabbage (from a
  2½- to 2¾-pound cabbage)
¾ cup firmly packed mayonnaise
¼ cup cider vinegar
2 tablespoons sugar
½ teaspoon salt or to taste

Place the cabbage in a large nonreactive bowl. Quickly whisk together the remaining ingredients, pour over the cabbage, and mix well. At first you may think that there isn't enough dressing, but the cabbage will release a fair amount of liquid. Let the slaw stand at room temperature for 30 minutes. Mix well, then cover and refrigerate for several hours. Stir the slaw well, taste for salt and adjust as needed, then serve as an accompaniment to fried chicken, fish or shellfish, or any kind of barbecue.

Makes 6 to 8 servings.

Apple-Raisin Coleslaw

¾ cup raisins

1 medium cabbage, grated

1 firm Red Delicious or
  Fuji apple, sliced and
  coarsely chopped

¼ cup mayonnaise

2 teaspoons sugar

2 teaspoons vinegar

½ teaspoon salt

Rinse the raisins under warm running water and pat dry with a paper towel. In a bowl, mix together the remaining ingredients. Taste for seasoning and adjust as necessary.

Serves 6 to 8.

Limas and Tomatoes

3 tablespoons bacon drippings or margarine

½ cup chopped sweet onions

1 small bag (10 ounces) frozen limas, cooked as directed

2 cans (14½ ounces each) stewed tomatoes, drained

Preheat oven to 350°. Heat the bacon drippings in a skillet and sauté the onions for 3 to 4 minutes. Stir in the limas and tomatoes and pour the mixture into a baking dish. Bake for 30 minutes.

Serves 6 to 8.

Corn Pudding

Silver corn is very popular for this dish.

½ stick butter or margarine
3 eggs, beaten
3 tablespoons flour
½ cup sugar

2 cups milk
4 cups fresh or frozen corn,
   thawed if frozen

Mix all the ingredients together in a bowl. Pour into a baking dish and bake for 1 hour at 350°.

Serves 6.

Tomato Juice Cocktail

This is a before meal "pick-me-up" often served in the sixties.

1 jar (46 ounces) tomato juice
2 tablespoons Worcestershire sauce
1 tablespoon lemon juice
3 teaspoons celery salt
few drops hot sauce

Mix and chill.

THE FOLLOWING recipes are great party food ideas.

Sausage Wheels

You can use turkey or pork sausage for this recipe.

1 pound bulk sausage
2 cups all-purpose flour
1 teaspoon baking powder

½ teaspoon salt
¼ cup shortening
about ⅔ cup milk

Have the sausage at room temperature. Combine the flour, baking powder, and salt in a bowl. Cut in the shortening and then add enough milk until it all comes together. Put the dough on a floured board and knead three times. Roll the dough out into a 16 × 12-inch rectangle. Spread the sausage on it, leaving a ½ inch on each end. Roll up jelly-roll fashion. Place the roll on a cookie sheet and refrigerate over night. Slice the roll into wheels about ¼ inch thick. Bake the wheels in a 350° oven for 12 minutes, until light brown.

Makes 15 to 20.

Egg Rolls

¼ stick butter
1 cup chopped shrimp
1 package bean sprouts
1 can (10 ounces) Chinese
   vegetables, drained

1 tablespoon soy sauce
1 cup finely shredded cabbage
1 package egg roll wrappers
1 egg, beaten

Heat the butter in a skillet until lightly browned. Add the shrimp, sprouts, and Chinese vegetables. Stir to mix well. Add the soy sauce and cook lightly. Add the cabbage, stirring to mix. Spoon the shrimp and vegetable mixture into the egg roll wrappers and roll up from a corner. Brush egg around the edge and seal. Fry in hot oil and drain on paper towels.

Makes 12.

Sweet and Sour Meatballs

½ pound ground beef
½ pound ground pork
2 onions, minced
1 teaspoon salt

½ cup grated Parmesan cheese
½ cup fine dry bread crumbs
1 egg, beaten
2 tablespoons cooking oil

Sauce

½ cup water
1 cup sugar
1 tablespoon soy sauce

1 teaspoon ketchup
2 tablespoons cornstarch
2 tablespoons water

Thoroughly mix together all of the meatball ingredients except the oil. Add a little water if the mixture seems dry. Shape the mixture into 16 balls. Heat the oil in a skillet over medium heat and brown the meatballs slowly.

To make the sauce, put the water, sugar, soy sauce, and ketchup in a small pot over low heat and bring to a boil. Stir the cornstarch into the water and pour into the sauce, slowly stirring until thickened. Pour the sauce over the meatballs to serve.

Serves 4 to 6.

Sweet and Sour Drumettes

1 cup brown sugar

1 large can (15¼ ounces) crushed pineapple, drained

⅔ cup soy sauce

¼ cup finely chopped sweet onions

3 tablespoons cornstarch

¼ cup water

1 cup cider vinegar

4 pounds chicken wings, cut at the joint to make drumettes (or purchase ready-cut drumettes)

Put the brown sugar, pineapple, soy sauce, and onions in a bowl. Combine the cornstarch and water and pour over the pineapple mixture, stirring to mix. Add the vinegar and chicken. Place the wings in a zipper lock bag or leave in the bowl and refrigerate for 45 minutes. Bake at 350° for 45 minutes, turning and stirring three times during cooking time. Check for tenderness.

Serves 8 to 10, 5 drumettes per serving.

Stuffed Mushrooms

Choose mushrooms that are about the same size and wipe them with a damp paper towel to clean.

12 medium mushrooms
¼ cup fresh bread crumbs, made
    from bread with the crusts
    removed
3 tablespoons grated Parmesan
    cheese

2 tablespoons butter
⅛ teaspoon granulated onion
½ teaspoon garlic salt

Preheat oven to 350°. Remove the stems from the mushrooms. Combine the other ingredients, mixing well, and spoon the mixture into the mushroom caps. Place on a greased baking sheet and bake for 25 to 30 minutes. Serve warm.

Serves 4.

Hamburger Pizza

½ pound ground beef
1 cup pizza sauce
1 12-inch prebaked pizza crust
3 cups shredded mozzarella cheese
¼ cup grated Parmesan cheese

Preheat oven to 450°. Brown the ground beef and drain off the fat. Spread the pizza sauce and beef over the crust. Cover with the mozzarella cheese and sprinkle the top with the Parmesan. Put on a pizza pan or cookie sheet and place on a low rack in the oven. Cook for 15 to 20 minutes until bubbling hot. Cut into slices to serve.

Serves 4.

Ham Pizza

1 12-inch prebaked pizza crust
1 tablespoon butter or margarine
1½ cups shredded ham
5 small tomatoes, sliced
½ teaspoon salt
2 cups shredded mozzarella cheese

Preheat oven to 400°. Brush the crust with butter. Spread the ham and sliced tomatoes on top. Sprinkle with the salt and spread the cheese over it. Put on a pizza pan or cookie sheet and place on a low rack in the oven. Bake about 15 minutes or until cheese melts.

Serves 4.

Vegetable Pizza

1 12-inch prebaked pizza crust
1 cup broccoli florets, sliced thin
1½ cups thinly sliced or chopped
   cauliflower
1 package (8 ounces) cream cheese
1 package (8 ounces) garden
   vegetable cream cheese
⅔ cup mayonnaise
1 teaspoon dried dill
1 teaspoon garlic salt
1 spring onion, thinly sliced
½ cup shredded carrot

Preheat oven to 400°. Put the pizza crust in the oven for about 10 minutes and then remove and let cool. Chill the broccoli and cauliflower in a bowl of ice water for 15 minutes; drain and pat dry. In a bowl, mix together the cream cheeses, mayonnaise, dill, garlic salt, and spring onion. Spread over the pizza crust. Press the vegetables onto the pizza. Refrigerate for 2 to 3 hours. Cut into 3-inch squares to serve.

Serves 4.

Cucumber-and-Onion-Filled Tomatoes

1 cucumber, finely chopped
1 medium onion, finely chopped
½ cup fresh basil, chopped

salt and black pepper to taste
4 ripe tomatoes

Combine the cucumber and onion with the basil, salt, and pepper. Core the tomatoes and stuff them with the cucumber and onion mixture. Refrigerate and serve topped with mayonnaise.

Serves 4.

Shrimp and Spinach Dip

1 pound shrimp, peeled
    and deveined
1 teaspoon garlic salt
1 teaspoon lemon juice
1 tablespoon vegetable oil

2 packages (8 ounces each) cream
    cheese, cut into slices
4 tablespoons milk
1 box (10 ounces) frozen chopped
    spinach, thawed

Cover the shrimp with water in a pot and add the garlic salt and lemon juice. Cook the shrimp until pink, then drain and set aside. Cook the oil, cream cheese, and milk over low heat until the cream cheese melt and the mixture is hot. Stir in the spinach and mix well. Put in a serving bowl and refrigerate until cool. Stir in the shrimp and refrigerate for 1 hour. When ready to serve, set the dip on a serving tray lined with crackers.

Shrimp Ball

1 stick butter, softened
1 package (8 ounces) cream cheese
   with chives, softened
1 tablespoon lemon juice
1 tablespoon mayonnaise
1 spring onion, sliced thin

3 cans (6 ounces each) shrimp,
   drained and chopped
½ teaspoon garlic salt
¼ teaspoon dried dill
black pepper (optional)

Blend the butter, cream cheese, lemon juice, and mayonnaise together.
Stir in the spring onion and shrimp to mix well. Add the salt, dill, and
black pepper. Press the mixture into a bowl lined with plastic wrap
or foil to form a ball. Refrigerate until firm or overnight. Place on a
serving dish lined with crackers.

Serves about 14 to 16.

Smoked Oyster Log

2 packages (8 ounces each) cream cheese, softened
2 tablespoons minced chives
3 cans (3 ounces each) smoked oysters in oil, with 2 tablespoons
   oil reserved

Put the cream cheese in a mixing bowl and mix until smooth. Add the
chives and the oil from the oysters and mix until combined. Line an
8-inch loaf pan with plastic wrap, allowing some of the wrap to hang
over the edge of the pan. Spread half of the cream cheese mixture
evenly across the bottom of the pan. Place the oysters over the cream
cheese mixture and then cover evenly with the remaining cheese
mixture. Chill for 2 hours or overnight.

Serves 8 to 10.

Clam Spread

2 packages (8 ounces each) cream cheese
1 can (4½ ounces) minced clams
2 tablespoons chopped celery
1 tablespoon dry mustard

Place the cream cheese in a mixing bowl and mix until smooth.
Add the remaining ingredients and mix until combined. Serve with
crackers.

Serves 8 to 10.

Spam Cheese Log

1 small can Spam, chopped
1 package (8 ounces) cream cheese
½ cup pecans, chopped fine
2 teaspoons sliced spring onions
¼ teaspoon Worcestershire sauce
chopped parsley

Combine all the ingredients and mix together well. Shape the mixture
into a log and wrap in wax paper; refrigerate to chill. Serve with
crackers or stuffed into tender celery.

Serves 6 to 8.

Dipping Sauce

This is a great sauce to dip vegetables or chips into.

1 cup mayonnaise
¼ cup ketchup
1 teaspoon horseradish
1 teaspoon Worcestershire sauce
¼ teaspoon garlic salt

Combine all the ingredients in a bowl and mix until well blended.

Serves 6.

Fun Dip

½ pound ground beef
1 jar (8 ounces) mild salsa
1 package taco seasoning mix
1 jar (8 ounces) Cheese Whiz
3 shakes hot sauce

Brown the ground beef in a frying pan over medium heat. Stir in the salsa, taco seasoning mix, and Cheese Whiz. Cover and cook on low heat, stirring often, until hot. Add the hot sauce. Serve with tortilla chips or toast rounds.

Serves 6.

Family Christmas Greeting Tray

My daughter Annette would make this tray and bring it to the family gathering at Christmas time.

lettuce

1 pineapple

1 small jar red maraschino cherries

1 small jar green maraschino cherries

2 dozen barbecue wings

1½ pounds cheese, cut into strips

1 large can low-sodium Spam, sliced

1 package pepper jack cheese squares

1 jar black olives

2 pounds grapes

2 cucumbers, cut into strips

Cover a large platter with lettuce leaves. Cut the top off the pineapple and place the top in the center of the platter. Put cherries in the pineapple top to make it look like a tree. Peel the pineapple and slice the fruit into chunks. Arrange the pineapple chunks and all the other ingredients around the pineapple top on the platter. Serve with hard crackers.

WE END THIS COOKBOOK where it all begins—with the children—and include recipes that they love to make. It's important to introduce cooking to children as early as possible. When they are making something that they love to eat, it keeps them interested in cooking.

Marshmallow Multigrain Cheerios Bar

1 cup butter or margarine
3 packages (10½ ounces each) miniature marshmallows
1 box Multigrain Cheerios

Combine the butter and marshmallows in the top of a double boiler and heat until the marshmallows melt, stirring occasionally. Fold in the cereal, and mix well to coat. Press the mixture into a lightly buttered 16 × 24-inch baking pan. Cool at room temperature approximately 1 hour and cut into desired serving size.

M&M Popcorn Balls

This is another kids' favorite.

2 cups sugar
½ cup light corn syrup
1½ cups water
1 tablespoon vanilla
5 quarts popped popcorn
1 package (24 ounces) plain
  chocolate M&Ms

Combine the sugar, corn syrup, and water in a saucepan and bring to a boil. Boil until the candy forms threads from a spoon dipped into the saucepan. Add the vanilla, remove the pan from the heat, and slowly pour the liquid over the popcorn in a large pan, turning the corn with a wooden spoon so that all of it is coated with the syrup. Form the popcorn into balls. Roll the balls in the M&Ms and wrap each one in waxed paper.

Index

Mixed summer squash, 158
Mountain Dew cake, 204
Muffins
blueberry-lemon muffins, 85
peach muffins, 86
pumpkin muffins, 85
sweet potato muffins, 84
Mullets, salt, 141
Mushrooms
meat loaf with horseradish and mushrooms, 103
peas, mushrooms, and rice bowl, 184
stuffed mushrooms, 266

1939 country wedding cake, 196
1950s community biscuit mix, 79
Noodle and vegetable casserole, 176
Norma's wedding cake top, 196
Nuts
apple-nut squares, 245
banana-pineapple-nut cake, 214
cranberry-nut bread, 83
cranberry-sweet potato-nut bread, 83
See also specific kinds of nuts

Okra
fried green tomato and okra patties, 152
pickled okra, 69
Old-fashioned apple pie, 232

Old-fashioned corned beef hash, 101
Old-fashioned lemon pound cake, 217
Onions
carrots, celery, onions, and raisins, 158
creamed green peas and onions, 163
cucumber-and-onion-filled tomatoes, 268
mixed greens and onions, 156
Oranges
orange cake, 207
orange cake layers, 208
orange cream cheese icing, 207
orange icing, 223
orange-pineapple salad, 72
orange-stuffed yams, 165
Oven-barbecued baby back ribs, 97
Oven chopped barbecue, 255
Oven-fried fish, 136
Oven-fried potatoes, 169
Oysters
fried oysters, 135
oyster bake, 139
oyster stew, 56
scalloped oysters, 136
smoked oyster log, 269

Pasta, sautéed mixed vegetables with, 180
Peas
fresh peas and corn, 160
See also Green peas

Peaches
fresh peach pie, 236
peach dessert, 250
peach muffins, 86
peach upside-down cake, 210
spiced peaches, 75
Pecans
chocolate pecan pie, 229
sweet potato-pecan-coconut pie, 230
Pickled okra, 69
Pickled pineapple, 75
Piecrust, 240
Pies
apple pie crumble, 233
chess pie, 226
chocolate pecan pie, 229
chocolate pie, 225
chocolate pie with cookie crust, 227
coconut cream pie, 228
coconut-pineapple pie, 229
French apple pie, 234
fresh peach pie, 236
lemon chess pie, 226
lemon meringue pie, 231
mince meat pie, 225
old-fashioned apple pie, 232
sweet potato–coconut pie, 237
sweet potato custard pie, 237
sweet potato-pecan-coconut pie, 230
sweet potato–pumpkin pie, 236
white potato pie, 238